GUIDE FOR THE CARE GIVER

by

DIANA S. DAVIS

Gotham Books

30 N Gould St.
Ste. 20820, Sheridan, WY 82801
https://gothambooksinc.com/

Phone: 1 (307) 464-7800

© 2024 *Diana S. Davis*. All rights reserved.

No part of this book may be reproduced, stored in a retrieval system, or transmitted by any means without the written permission of the author.

Published by Gotham Books (March 14, 2024)

ISBN: 979-8-88775-821-3 (P)
ISBN: 979-8-88775-822-0 (E)

Because of the dynamic nature of the Internet, any web addresses or links contained in this book may have changed since publication and may no longer be valid.

The views expressed in this work are solely those of the author and do not necessarily reflect the views of the publisher, and the publisher hereby disclaims any responsibility for them.

Contents

Acknowledgement vii

Introduction... ix

COVID 19 Virus.. xii

Chapter 1

   The Care Giver...1

Chapter 2

   Alzheimer's Disease and Dementia..................................5

Chapter 3

   Amputation or Loss of Limb 10

      Wound Care Instructions 13

      Bed Bath 15

      Washing The Private Part of A Man And A Woman ..17

      For women..18

      For Men 19

      The Slider-Board 20

Chapter 4

   Cancer 22

Chapter 5

Cerebral Palsy 27

Chapter 6

   Diabetes 33

      How To Take A Gucose Test 36

Chapter 7

    Grief 38

Chapter 8

    Heart Attack 42

        How To Take A Blood Pressure 47

Chapter 9

    Parkinson's Disease 50

        Lifting Your Client/Patient 56

Chapter 10

    Stroke 63

        The Symptoms Of A Stroke 66

        Turning The Client/Patint 79

        To Move The Client Towards The Headboard 80

Chapter 11

    Surgeries 87

Chapter 12

    Vertigo and Dizziness 93

Chapter 13

    Virus 98

Chapter 14

    Death 104

Chapter 15

    Documentation 117

        Documentation Journal 121

        Prayer of Saint Francis of Assisi 124

Chapter 16

Help for the Care Giver 125

    Injuries on the Job 141

Chapter 17

    Meditations 144

        Breathing Meditation 146

        Walking Meditation 146

        Singing Meditation 147

        Meditative Dancing 147

        Progressive Relaxation Meditation 148

Chapter 18

    Affirmations 151

My Biography 155

Resources 159

Recommended Reading 161

My Journal 162

I Dedicate this book to
Charles Reynolds Woolfenden

My husband and best friend that I had in life.
May he rest in peace.

ACKNOWLEDGEMENT

I wish to acknowledge all the people who have helped me with my book, "Guide for the Care Giver," from the beginning up until now.

Dana Traver, thank you for all of your help in helping me and encouraging me to decide to start writing another book.

Carolyn Morrison, thank you for your trusting me and believing in me. I am very grateful for your friendship, your wisdom, and your intuition.

Brett Adams, thank you for your patience, in keeping in contract with me, for a year before I made the decision to write this book. You helped me have the courage to do this great work of art, word, and beauty that is in this book. Thank you for proof-reading my manuscript and guiding me on the proper grammar to write this book. You are truly a dear friend to me.

Lorraine Heoptner, thank you for your friendship, wisdom, and encouraging me to write my first book, and also my second book. You are my best friend and fan of all my books.

Gotham Books, I thank all of the professional artists, the designers, and the work you have done for the cover of my book. Thank you to the people that formatted, and arranging the chapters in my book.

I thank God, for helping and guiding me while writing this book.

INTRODUCTION

Care giving has become the fastest growing need for the large population of the elderly people. Most of the elderly group of people are between sixty-five to the age of the nineties and now on up to the century mark of the age of one-hundred years old or more.

Most of the many people who are in the group of the Baby Boomer generation are now in the elderly group. Those that were born between the years of 1946 to the year of 1964, are rapidly entering into the senior citizen group, and are walking in the elderly group of America, and also the world.

Another group of people that are needing help, and needing a care giver are the military veterans. They are coming home from doing his or her tour of duty fighting in wars around the world, in war torn countries and where there is a lot of conflicts. Many of the veterans have serious, and challenging injuries. The veterans have become handicap because of the injuries they have sustain in a war situation.

This book is for all families, each member of the family. This book is for all care givers be that they are doctors, nurses, men, women, children, clergy of all faiths, and nationalities. Care givers give care without boundaries. Care givers can be of any age, from a young child to a very old senior citizen.

One of the best care givers, in the world, to my opinion was a Catholic nun by the name of Mother Teresa of Calcutta, India. She gave her heart, love, and care giving skills to the humanity of the sick, the dyeing, and the poor of the poorest people in India. Mother Teresa's example of this great capacity to care for people is the reason why I was able to work so long in the care giving field.

In this book, "Guidance for the care giver", I explain how to efficiently and joyously take care of people, and families that need help from a care giver.

In the year 2015, I had a dream that I was to write a book about care giving and helping people understand how to take care of people. To discuss through the words contained in this book, the ways to take care of the client/patient, yet the care giver will learn how to take care of herself/himself.

This book will discuss how to protect yourself from getting hurt while on the job. I want to share with you, my readers, the easiest and healthiest ways to do the care giving work, and enjoy doing it. I also want to give you the best information and suggestions, and my secrets of surviving the many hours, days, and weeks, and years, working the long shifts of taking care of your client/patient.

You will learn about the different common diseases and illnesses. I will list them in an alphabetical order and explain the basic meaning of each disease and illness. Then I will explain to you how to take care of the client/patient. I also offer some chapters on how to take care of yourself and your needs. I will help you understand why you may feel stressed and burned out. I will help you learn how to be positive and creative with your job as a care giver, and how to enjoy doing your work as a care giver while taking care of the elderly, the sick, the disabled, and also the dying patient/client.

I will speak about the person as, "client/patient."

I will refer them or they as he/she, his/her. The reason for this is because people feel an offence about gender related thought and things.

This book is for all ages, genders, relationships, and family. Also, the medical community, rest homes for the sick, and the recovery facilities. For the Hospice nursing, and care giving.

COVID 19 VIRUS

In the beginning of the year of 2020, there was a world-wide pandemic that shook the world and literally stopped all businesses from being open for business, and all churches of all religions were closed to worship together in a building. The people could not be outside in public, and the governments from all over the world put a mandatory, "stay at home," law to stop the people from mingling among each other because of the pandemic illness.

This pandemic name is, "Covid Nineteen Virus." This virus started in China. The people in China got ill and also the people that came to China from all over the world. There were many flights in and out of China that carried many passengers. When the people took plane flights home to his/her country, unbeknown to these people they were ill with the Covid Nineteen virus, and this deadly, very contagious virus came to the families, neighbors, friends, and co-workers from the person that was coming back home from China. The Cova Nineteen Virus spread throughout the world, starting from the East, North, West, and South. By the end of the year of 2020, most every part of the planet, and the people was suffering the symptoms, illness, extreme sickness, and many people died from the deadly Covid Nineteen Virus.

There were many sudden changes in the way of life. People panicked, they bought cleaning supplies, every kind of paper goods, especially toilet paper. Quickly all the retail stores ran out of all paper goods that pertained to cleaning, disinfecting, and toiletries. So, the shelves in the stores were empty. To walk into these stores, and see the empty shelves baron without any paper goods, this was very disheartening and yes scarry.

The effects of the forced confinement, were showing up in the population, and the result of all the confinement and isolation. The people had to endure, behaviors of fears, anger, grief, and feeling so sick, manifesting in behaviors that American people have never felt would happen to them.

The hospitals across the world, in every nation, country, were full to the maximum capacity of people, getting treatment and help from the doctors. It wasn't just the people getting sick with the Covid Nineteen Virus but also the hospital personnel, were getting sick too. Doctors, nurses, specialists, and the cleaning people, on down to the least expected person got sick. This group of people was the first responders to take care of the massive amount of people that flowed through the hospital doors.

Many of the first responders from the hospitals got sick and died from the pandemic world sickness.

Many of the people that was in care homes, and rest homes got sick with the deadly sickness of Covid Nineteen Virus. The patients and clients had the care givers that came into the rest homes, and the care homes to take care of the clients, and patients. Unbeknown to the care giver, the Covid Nineteen Virus was rapidly going through the people, the patient/client. Many care givers got sick, and many of them died from the sickness of Covid Nineteen Virus complications.

To this day, October, 2023, Covid Nineteen Virus is still with us.

CHAPTER 1

The Care Giver

*Blessed are the peacemakers, for they
Shall be called the children of God.
Matthew 5:9 kjv.*

What is a care giver? A caregiver is a person who attends to the personal needs of people, such as children, the sick and the dying, the elderly, and people who have physical and mental disabilities. Care givers give a lot of nurturing care, with a lot of compassion and love. They can be a woman or a man. A care giver can be a family member, a doctor, a nurse, a governess, a babysitter, a nanny, a companion, a guardian, or an attendant.

The care giver's day starts early in the morning, before the client wakes up. When you get up in the morning, always take a shower, and get dressed for the day. Wear clothes that are comfortable to wear. Try to find clothing that has pockets on the sides of the shirt and pants. Pockets are a life saver and convenient. Pockets are handy to put things in when you are working with your client/patient.

Be professional and courteous in your actions and doing your job while you are working.

Always document the days happenings in the client's/patient's document journal. There is an example of a document journal in the back of the book.

The care giver starts the day by getting all the medications ready for the client/patient to take either before or after breakfast. The client/patient is assisted as he/she gets out of bed and takes a shower or a sponge bath, the male client/patient has his face shaved either by himself or the care giver can shave his face. The client/patient will comb his/her hair, or the care giver can do this for the client/patient. Have the clothes ready, to help your client/patient get dressed for the day.

Putting on the clothes and shoes takes time to do. The care giver will help and assist in dressing the client/patient. If the client/patient can't dress himself/herself. Always start with the weakest part of the body, and end with the stronger part of the body.

During mealtimes, the client/patient may have to wear a bib to help keep his/her clothes clean. This is likely due to the fact that the client/patient may not be able to hold food or liquids in his/her mouth because of weakness of the muscles around the mouth. The client's/patient's saliva will often drool onto the bib. Some clients/patients will spit his/her food out, and the food will fall on the bib.

There are a lot of different kinds of protection for client's and patient's clothing. The bib I like the best covers from the neck to the waist, and it has a pocket across the bottom of the bib. On the neckline, the ties attach in the back of the neck, with Velcro brand attachment tabs.

When the client/patient eats, you as the care giver, need to be aware of how the client/patient is eating, and whether he/she is choking on the food. Sometimes you will have to assist in feeding your client/patient who may not be able to hold a cup, a spoon, or a fork in his/her hand. Also be sure there is a cup of water for your client/patient to drink. You may have to assist in holding the glass of water or another beverage for your client/patient to drink.

After your client/patient is finished eating his/her meal, you may have to clean the client's/patient's hands, the face, and mouth. If the client/patient can do this himself/herself let them, do it.

During the day, many things have to be done, such as light housekeeping, fixing meals, washing clothes and changing the bedding. The care giver needs to be vigilant in paying attention to the client/patient at all times. Sometimes you will have an active client/patient who likes to wander around and get into things that are inside the house that he/she are not supposed to get into, or the client/patient might get outside, and decides to take a walk by himself/herself. This can be a dangerous situation, and you must keep on top of this.

Many times, the care giver is also a companion to the client/patient. This is a common reason why care givers are needed. Elderly clients and patients get lonely and are afraid to be alone. Being a companion is a rewarding experience. You may become friends with your client/patient, and you may do many things together, such as working in the flower garden, going outside and taking walks, having time to go shopping and eating out. Clients and patients love doing this. Even go for a scenic drive in the mountains, or drive through the pretty parts of town. Other things you can do are play card games, do puzzles putting them together, friends of your client/patient may invite you and your client/patient to come to birthday parties or to visit. In general, just be positive and happy. Remember to smile. Surprisingly a smile makes people feel better.

CHAPTER 2

Alzheimer's Disease and Dementia

My little children let us love, not in word, or speech, but and in truth and action.
1 John 3:18

Alzheimer's Disease is a condition in which the brain cells deteriorate and die. The brain loses the ability to process new information, or store and retrieve old and new memories. Alzheimer's disease steadily gets worse as time passes. Alzheimer's Disease is a fatal disease that the memory will never be restored.

Dementia is a slow progressive memory loss that can be restored through doing different mental and physical exercises, such as doing word puzzles, playing board-games, card games, catch the ball, playing sports, and general exercises.

Alzheimer's Disease and Dementia are both dealing with memory loss. They involve a brain disorder that is similar to senility and extreme forgetfulness. As the years go by, the memory gets worse. Symptoms typically start showing up in the middle sixties, but it can begin in the client's/patient's thirties and forties. The symptoms manifest as forgetting recent events. Anything that takes concentration is difficult for the client/patient to do. Another noticeable thing is forgetting or not recognizing people and the people's name. Tasks such as choosing clothing, personal grooming and hygienically keeping clean can become very challenging and frustrating to the client/patient. In the advanced stage of Alzheimer's Disease, there is complete loss of memory, speech, and muscle function.

Many people who have Alzheimer's Disease and/or dementia do not realize he/she has the problem, and he/she are in denial about this much of the time. He/she will repeat the same subject over and over for long periods of time during the day. Many people with memory loss that have been in a war situation will repeatedly reminisce about his/her experience. The memory reminisces get deeper and deeper into the past as the client/patient speaks about the experience that was happening to him/her. This is also true with other memories of marriages, and traumatic events. It all depends on how recent the event was. As time goes by, people will lose all of his/her memories, and eventually including all the names of the family, friends, grandchildren, husband and/or wife.

How do you, as the care giver, take care and help someone who is forgetful, and repeating the same conversation? What can be helpful to you, the care giver, in dealing with someone who have this problem, and what are the best solutions for this?

1. The first thing you can do is just let the client/patient talk about what is on his/her mind. You can also listen to what he/she is saying, without interrupting the client/patient. This will help you have a clue and an understanding of what the client/patient is feeling and worrying about. Reassure the client/patient that he/she is safe, and that all the worrisome matters will be resolved soon. It takes a lot of patience on your part to answer all the repeated questions.
2. Forgetful clients and patients have a lot of fears that include the safety of their bodies, the safety of their belongings, and the safety of their homes.

How can you reassure your client/patient that he/she is safe? If the client/patient is able to walk and move around, let him/her show you what it is that is bothering him/her. For example: walk with your client/patient when it comes time to lock up the house for the night. Close all the windows that need to be closed shut. Close the blinds and curtains so that there will be privacy for everyone in the house. Maybe you can make a schedule of the things to do at night and the client/patient can sign his/her check-mark on the schedule. Be sure you date it and sign it. This will save you a lot of anxiety and worry when dealing with these stressing issues with your client/patient.

3. Money fears are a major concern for clients/patients. Financial security is the most important thing to the client/patient.
4. Clients/patients will feel that they do not need any care giver's help, and question why you are there in the first place. The client/patient will argue and try to make you feel bad and embarrass you. If you need to contact the power of attorney for the client/patient and explain to them about your client's/patient's concern about you the care giver being there. Have the power of attorney talk to the client/patient to reassure that he/she is safe to have a care giver.
5. Thieving clients/patients. This is a major concern to the care giver. Many care givers have had clients/patients go through the care giver's suitcase, and steal money, hair brushes and combs, jewelry, craft supplies, like knitting needles, crochet hooks, books and even the care giver's underwear. I'm not kidding you. This has happened to me on several occasions

while I took care of clients/patients.
6. The behavior of Alzheimer's clients/patients can be erratic at times. He/she can be calm and nice, and then all of a sudden, he/she will be in a rage and suddenly hit you hard on the face, sometimes you will fall on the floor. So, my advice to you is always be prepared for any kind of thing that can happen to you but also with the client/patient. Always report this kind of behavior to your supervisor or the power of attorney of the client's/patient's behavior. With a client/patient like this, you must take frequent brakes and get calmed down. Breathe, and drink water. Let the client calm down and try not to talk too much with him/her for a little while. You don't need to argue or fight with your client/patient. It doesn't help the situation.
7. When you take on a new patient or a client, be sure you find out what kind of temperament, and/or behaviors that the client/patient have. If it is a man or a woman. Just remember you need to feel safe at the job. Do not except a job if you feel threatened, scared or unsure of the job. Your safety is the most important thing to remember. You are not there to take care of that person for him/her to hit you, or unhinge you in any way, and psychologically demean you or hurt you. You have the rights to work in a safe job and place.

CHAPTER 3

Amputation or Loss of Limb

*He gives power to the faint; and to them that
Have no might, he increases strength.
Isaiah 40:29 kjv.*

An amputation of a loss of a limb involves the removal of a diseased part of the body due to the injuries caused from accidents, automobile accidents, injuries caused from weapons like knives, guns, swords, and bow-arrows.

Other reasons for an amputation are from diseases like diabetes from sugar being too high. Diabetes can cause infection and ulcerated sores that get infected and if not treated gang-green sets in. Gang-green kills the flesh and it will spread to other parts of the body. If left untreated you will die. Amputation is the usual way to get rid of gang-green by cutting off parts of the body such as toes, feet, part of the leg, or all of the leg. Arms, and hands can get gang-green, and they too can be amputated.

After the surgery of an amputation, the client/patient will have to be sedated with medication until the pain subsides, and the patient/client will be able to communicate.

The client/patient needs to be calm while he/she is recovering from surgery. The wound needs to be kept clean and watched to ensure there is no infection or complications occurring in the areas near the site of the surgery area, such as swelling and redness that could be showing blood poisoning and infection like puss that looks creamy white and sticky.

Bandages need to be changed on a regular schedule, and also the cleaning of the wound.

There should be instructions with the list of what to do after a surgery that your client/patient received from the hospital release papers, if not call the doctor's office and speak to the nurse. The doctor's orders should be done exactly like the doctor wants done on the wound. If there is a question on any part of the procedure of cleaning a wound, please be sure you call the doctor's nurse that is in charge of this patient/client.

When you change a wound bandage, be sure you have all of the cleaning solutions to clean the wound, the antibacterial ointments or salves to put onto the wound. Also make sure you have the right size bandage ready to put onto the wound. Have all of these wound care supplies available to get to when there is an emergency. If there is blood coming through the bandages from the wound, immediately change that bandage.

When I was taking care of patients that had wounds, I asked the visiting nurses from the Hospice care to teach me how to care for wounds. So, I'm letting you know you can ask the visiting nurses to help you. The nurses are so happy to help you learn how to take care of your client/patient, and it shows the nurses that you really do care about the health of your client/patient. Below are some wound care instructions to follow.

WOUND CARE INSTRUCTIONS

1. Put on rubber or plastic gloves before touching the patient. This will protect the patient from receiving any infections, and it protects you from receiving any kind of a blood transferred disease.
2. Have a table near the place where you will be cleaning the wound. The table will need a paper towel set on it before you put the tools and bandage materials on the table. Then put the tools and bandage materials, ointments and/or salves, cleaning solution to clean the wound, sterilized scissors and sterilized tweezers, also sterilized gauze to help you clean the wound. You will also need a trash receptacle with a trash bag inside of it to put the soiled bandages into it.
3. Have the patient/client lie down on a table or a bed. Before the patient/client lies down onto the bed, make sure you have a water-soluble pad, (a chuck) under the client's/patient's wound, so that the chuck will catch all the liquids and blood on it. If the patient/client is sitting at a table, put a chuck on the table surface then put the wound part of the patient on the covered table chuck to clean the wound.
4. Gently remove the bandage from the wound. You may have to use the sterilized tweezer to

pick up the bandage on a bloody or dried blood spot and carefully lift the bandage away from the wound and throw the bandage in the trash receptacle. Take a sterilized gauze pad to lightly touch the wound to dry up any kind of blood or serum- like liquids. If there is puss use the sterilize pad to remove the puss on top of the wound.
5. Wash the wound with the wound cleaning solution; if there is no wound-cleaning solution, you can use no soap cleaning solution, dilute it in sterilized water. Take your time doing this process, don't rush through this. Be gentle, as there can be pain that the client/patient is experiencing.
6. Put the antibacterial ointment or salve onto the wound. Use a Q-tip to apply the ointment or solve onto the wound.
7. Place the sterilized gauze onto the wound. Then cover the gauze with a bandage covering such as a stretch-bandage cover tape.
8. Be sure you record this procedure in the Documentary Journal. The time, you changed the bandages, and also your observance of the healing process of the wound.

Be aware of the client's/patient's need to talk and release his/her deep feelings from dealing with the loss of the limb that he/she has experienced. Sometimes the client/patient may feel like the limb is still there on his/her body. There will be a lot of pain, depression, and crying. Be compassionate, listen to your client/patient without interruptions, and ending or trying to finish the client's/patient's sentence. This is rude and unacceptable behavior on the care giver's part.

When a client/patient has had an amputation, he/she could be bed-bound. I recommend the use of a bed-bath. It is difficult to move a client/patient on and off a bed or a wheelchair when there is a lot of soreness, and pain that the client/patient is suffering with.

BED BATH

Before you do a bed-bath, you must have a table next to the bed with a towel on the table to catch the water if it splashes out of the bed-bath tub. Heat up the water to make it warm and put the water and no-soap liquid into the bed-bath tub. Place the tub onto the table beside the bed. Have two to three large towels, and two hand towels, and have two or three water absorbing pads, (Chucks). Undress the client/patient and cover him/her with a large towel so that he/she will not get chilled. Start at the head to clean the client/patient and end cleaning at the private part of the body. The private part of the body is the penis, on the man, and the vaginal area of the body of the woman. It is recommended that the Client/patient clean his/her own private part of his/her body.

Put a chuck under the client/patient before you start washing the body. Remember the chuck is a pad that absorbs the water, and it keeps the bed dry.

Wash the head and face first, then take the towel and dry the head. Go down to the arms and wash the arms and hands, then take a towel and dry the arms and hands. Go down to the chest or breast area and gently wash that area. Take a towel and dry that area. Put a dry towel across the chest area to keep the client/patient warm. Go down to the stomach and hips and wash that area, take a towel, and dry that area. Cover the client/patient with a towel to keep the client/patient warm. Before you turn the client/patient, pull out the wet chuck from underneath the client/patient. Put a dry chuck under the client/patient as you turn him/her onto his/her stomach. Continue to turn the client/patient over, onto his/her stomach so that you can wash the back. After you wash and dry the back, cover the client/patient with a dry towel. Go down to the buttocks and clean the buttocks, dry the buttocks with a towel and cover the client with a dry towel. Go down to the legs and clean the legs and feet, take a towel, and dry the legs and feet. Turn the client/patient on his/her side and pull out the wet chuck. Replace another clean dry chuck under the client/patient, then move the client/patient onto his/her back. Have the client/patient clean his/her privates. While the client/patient is cleaning his/her private area, please give him/her the dignity of privacy by taking a towel and hold it in front of him/her were you the care giver are not looking at the client/patient. Let me tell you, this is very embarrassing to the client/patient and also embarrassing to you the care giver.

After you are done washing the client/patient. It is time for him/her to get dressed, or you can put a clean nightgown for the woman, or a clean tea shirt on the man. I always suggest this when clients/patents are bedbound.

WASHING THE PRIVATE PART OF A MAN AND A WOMAN

When you wash the client's/patient's private area you must get his/her permission to wash and clean your him/her. Once you have the approval of your client/patient then you can wash and clean him/her.

Be careful and respectful when you clean the private parts of the client's/patient's body. Respect the privacy that your client/patient. Always remember to wash the private front to back. Put a chuck underneath the back hips between the waist and the thighs. Have the buttocks sit in the center of the chuck.

For women

With a woman you need to wash the front part of her private part of her body. Use a lot of water and non-soap liquid body cleaner in the water tub. Use a soft rag or a throwaway rag to wash the sensitive parts and the vaginal opening. If there is stool, fesses, poop, on or around the vagina opening you will have to use toilet paper or a cleaning wipe to clean out the stool. Wipe a spot at a time, wipe, throw away the wipe away into the trash receptacle, get another wipe and continue to wipe off the stools until there is none on the body. Then use the cleaning water with a rag to wash off the vaginal opening and the area around it. When you wash the rectum, anus area, have the client/patient lift her hips off the bed and spread her legs apart so that you can clean the rectum, buttocks, and the surrounding area. Dry off the surrounding area and pull out the wet chuck and throw it into the trash receptacle. Now you can put on clean under panties on your client/patient.

For Men

With a man, you will wash the scrotal bag first and then the penis. Make sure that you gently pull the foreskin away from the head of the penis so you can clean any urine or stools from the foreskin and head of the penis. Be careful, this is a very sensitive area and can be painful. Use lots of water and non-soap wash.

After you wash the private parts of a man and clean the anus/rectum area and buttocks, you can throw away the wet chuck in the trash receptacle. You can now put on clean underpants on the client/patient.

You must be strong and believe in yourself that you can do this. Keep remembering that you are doing a service for the clients/patients good. I assure you that you will be blessed through performing and doing this compassionate service with kindness and love of humanity.

The client/patient may have to take certain medications. You must be aware of the schedule for when medication have to be given to the client/patient. Always keep a Document journal or a log book as to when you give the medications to your client/patient. Always document everything you do when you are working at the job site.

If you are a care giver that works for an agency, find out if your employer gives you the permission to give medications to the client/patient. I say this because there are laws that prevent care givers dispensing medications, unless the care giver has permission to do this. Always remember being aware of these things. Keep an open communication with the family member who is in charge of the client/patient. If you have feelings or thoughts and concerns about your job and the client, always let your employer know about this. The reason for this could be a legal situation so you must cover your back, so to speak.

THE SLIDER-BOARD

To transfer an amputee client/patient, you will need a slider-board. This is a board that is twelve to eighteen inches wide by thirty-six inches long, some slider-boards can be made longer if it is needed. Slider-boards are used a lot to transfer a client/patient that has had a leg amputation. Use the slider board so that the client/patient can slide on the board from the bed to the wheelchair. The slider-board can be used in various other transfer uses such as to transfer to furniture, in and out of an automobile.

If the client/patient is clothed and dressed, he/she can be transferred to the wheelchair. Put the slider-board end of the board on the bed, and put the other end of the slider-board on the wheelchair seat. Make sure you take off the armrest of the wheelchair, so that you can put the slider-board on the seat. Then you are ready to transfer the client/patient. Have the client/patient sit on the slider-board. Help the client/patient slide sideways, moving toward the wheelchair. Maneuver the client/patient into the seat of the wheelchair so that he/she is sitting comfortably in the seat. Take the slider-board out from underneath the client/patient, and put it by the bed or against a wall. Replace the armrest back onto the wheelchair.

If there is a problem that the clothes or the skin is sticking to the slider-board put some baby powder on it. This will make the slider-board slippery so that the client/patient can move across the slider-board easily. This method of transferring a client/patient can be used in most all transfering situations.

CHAPTER 4

Cancer

To everything there is a season, and a time
To every purpose under the heaven.
Ecclesiastes 3:1. Kjv.

Cancer is an abnormal growth that grows within the body or on the outer parts of the body. The abnormal growth is irregular in shape. It is also called a tumor, or a mutation of the cells. Cancer can appear anywhere on the body, inside or outside of the body. Cancer can grow on any bone, organs, or tissues, and can spread from one spot to another spot inside the body or on the skin of the body.

Clients/patients who have cancer or have had cancer surgery will need care giving and a care giver will need to assist the client/patient with the care that he/she needs. You will be helping the client/patient back onto his/her feet and out of bed if the client/patient can move out of bed.

The healing from a cancer surgery can take a long time to heal. Clients/patients may have to see the doctor and physical therapist many times, and receive treatments such as Chemotherapy and/or Radiation treatments. Chemotherapy is the use of chemical agents by a shot to control and get rid of the cancer cells that are still on the tissues inside the body. Radiation therapy is the use of radiation energy waves going through the skin into the body part that has the cancer and burning the cancer cells out of the tissues of the body. These two types of treatments will stop the growth of the cancer cells from multiplying and starting another growth in another part of the body. This is also a preventative treatment so that cancer will not come back into the body.

The side effects of chemotherapy and radiation have many symptoms, such as nausea, vomiting, diarrhea, headaches, hair loss, burning on the skin from the radiation treatment, bleeding, anemia, immune system weakened, scaring on the skin and inside the body where the surgery was performed on.

The reason that I am listing the symptoms that the client/patient is experiencing is because you, the care giver, must know how to take care of the client/patient. The care giver needs to know what to do when the symptoms show up and when to call the doctor's office for help, and report the symptoms that the client/patient is having. You may have to put medication salves or ointments on the radiation burn sites on the client's/patient's skin. You will have to be observant of the behavior and the emotions of the client/patent, and how he/she is feeling. Ask your client/patient, "how are you feeling, what is worrying you, and what do you need? "Are you in pain? Where is the pain at?" Make sure you document this in the Document Journal.

Home nurses will come and check on the status of the client/patient. If it is ok with the visiting nurses, ask them if you can stay to observe how the nurses take care of the client's/patient's wounds and other processes that have to be done.

Sometimes you will have a client/patient come home with drainage tubing sticking outside of the body where the surgery was performed. The tubing has a drainage shut off point to open to drain the accumulated liquids from the surgery sight. You may have to drain the tube. So, ask the nurses to show you how to do this. I guarantee you will be learning a valuable lesson on caring for your client/patient.

The care giver must be extra careful about how he/she helps the client/patient that is in a lot of pain, and is suffering a lot of mental and emotional distress. Try to be compassionate and caring to the client/patient. Be there to listen to the client and offer a kind word. Try not to touch the client/patient too much as he/she may hurt all over his/her body. The client will be sensitive and sometime a bit crabby. Let the client talk it out and release his/her feelings and emotional hurts. It's ok for them to do this. It helps to relieve the pain, and also the fear the client/patient is experiencing.

The doctor will send the client/patient home with a simple diet or a routine to follow. You must follow the doctor's order as prescribed. When you cook meals, make it easy on yourself. Less can be better. The appetite of the client/patient may be nominal, but the appetite will gradually come back, and the client/patient will eat better, and also feel better.

If you, the care giver, feel a lot of stress and tension, just stop what you are doing, you need to do some de-stressing exercises and start deep-breathing more. Oxygen in the body, helps the body relax. When you forget to breathe, you lose oxygen, and you will feel confused, tired, and stressed. Breathing makes you relax and feel calmer. Meditation and affirmations will help you from having negative feelings and it will help you have your sense of self-esteem in order. There is a chapter later in the book that has Meditations and affirmations to help you.

CHAPTER 5

Cerebral Palsy

*It is you who light my lamp;
The Lord, my God
Lights up my darkness.
Psalm 18:28 NRSV.*

This picture is a water color freeform painting. By Diana Davis

Cerebral Palsy is a disorder caused by brain damage, usually before the baby is born, or when the baby is born, or shortly after the birth of the baby. The baby will have a defective muscle control problem in his/her body. The baby will not be able to control his/her movements with the arms and hands, and the legs and feet. The head of the body will shake, or move in uncontrolled positions. The eyes will move shakily and unfocused.

The Cerebral Cortex in the brain is the surface layer of the gray-mater of the Cerebrum, (look at the highlighted purple in the illustration), that functions chiefly in coordination of the sensory and motor information. This is basically saying that the Cerebral Cortex controls all of the muscles and nerves of the body, and the sense to feel and touch with the fingers and skin.

The Cerebellum, (also called the Little Brain), (look at the highlighted navy-blue in the illustration), is the part of the brain that projects over the medulla and is concerned especially with the coordination of the muscular action, and with bodily balance. This basically is saying that the Cerebellum controls the coordination and movement of the action of the muscles, and the Cerebellum helps to keep the body balanced, so that you will not fall and hurt yourself.

The Medulla Oblongata is the connection between the brainstem and the spinal cord, carrying multiple important functional centers.

(look at the highlighted yellow in the illustration). It is comprised of the cardiovascular respiratory regulation system, the descending motor tracts, the ascending sensory tracts, and the origin of cranial nerves. This is saying that the Medulla Oblongata controls the cardiovascular respiratory area of the body. The cardiovascular is dealing with the heart. The respiratory is dealing with the lungs. So, when you breathe you take in oxygen into the lungs, and the oxygen goes to the heart, and the heart feeds on the oxygen to keep it going. The Medulla Oblongata also controls the motor function of the muscles, and the ascending sensory tract controls the sense of feeling things. The Medulla Oblongata controls the nerves in the large nerve area close to the base of the brain, called the Brainstem.

The Cerebrum is the enlarged front and upper part of the brain, (look at the highlighted green in the illustration), and it contains the upper center area. The largest part of the brain, the Cerebrum, initiates and coordinates movement and regulates temperature. Other areas of the Cerebrum enable speech, judgement, thinking and reasoning, problem solving, emotions, and learning. Other functions relate to vision, hearing, touch, and other senses.

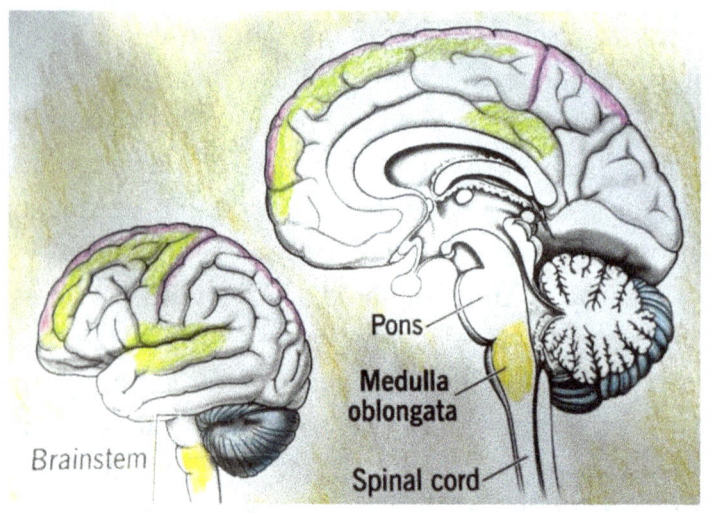

Cerebral Palsy is a neurological disorder of the brain and causes the body movements not to move in the smooth flowing movements. The body has a slow movement that jerks and has uncontrollable movement on the extremities such as the arms, hands, and the legs and feet. The head moves and shakes uncontrollably. The speech is affected because the control is not working between the muscle and the speech process in the brain. The mouth muscles are weak, and the fluids in the mouth are not contained in the mouth because the lips drop and the saliva drool out of the mouth, and falls on the client's/patient's chest. Use a bib to cover the upper chest. This will help to keep the clothes around the chest area clean. Keep extra bibs available just in case you need to change the bibs often.

Incontinence happens when the client/patient can't hold his/her urine and stools, (poop). The client/patient can't feel that he/she needs to go urinate or use the toilet to release the stools into the toilet. The client/patient will feel embarrassed when he/she loses control of his/her bowels, and bladder. The client/patient will have to wear a diaper, either a cloth diaper, or a disposable-pull up diaper. The care giver will have to be observant, and check the diaper often to be sure the client's/patient's diaper is dry, and if it needs to be changed. It is very important that the diaper gets changed often as the dampness from the urine will irritate the skin, and cause sores on the skin.

The client/patient will have to be turned often because resting for a long time in bed, in one position causes compression on the skin, and the skin will bruise and become a bedsore. Bedsores are very painful to have, and they can cause infection. There are bedsore salves or creams that can be used to relive the pain from a bedsore.

The care giver or a family member will have to help feed the client/patient. When you feed a person, you need to be gentle in putting the spoon or fork into the mouth. Especially when you are using a fork, as the fork has sharp prongs. You need to be patient and go slow when feeding the client/patient. Have a towel or a washrag handy just in case you need to clean up any messes, from food falling out of the client's/patient's mouth. After you are done feeding the client/patient, remove the bib and wash off his/her face and hands.

The client/patient will have to have a care giver for the rest of his/her life. He/she will have good days and bad days. Each day try to take the client/patient outside for walks. You will push the wheelchair. There are also electric wheelchairs that can be used as well. Fresh air, and just being outside is invigorating, and good for both you and the client/patient. Watching television is really great to do with a client/patient as he/she will enjoy seeing and hearing what is on the television. This will also help occupy and interest the client/patient so that there will be no problem dealing with boredom or having nothing to do.

CHAPTER 6

DIABETES

*Blessed are they which do hunger and thirst
After righteousness for they shall be filled.
Matthew 5:6 kjv.*

Diabetes is a disease that is caused by too much sugar in the blood; the pancreas can't produce enough insulin to metabolize the sugar in the blood. Diabetes can be hereditary, and it runs through the family ancestry for many generations. Many people have it as small children, and people who get older. They can have type two diabetes as adults.

Many people are on medications to control insulin levels, which are monitored by using a glucometer to test the blood sugar levels. This helps to identify the insulin dosage, as per the doctor's order. A blood count number informs the person about how much he/she can eat for the day. Sometimes the blood might need to be tested later in the day as well. People who have diabetes have to take medication to keep his/her blood glucose in a lower number range. Some people can use the diabetic diet, and watching what he/she eats during the day that will help keep the blood glucose levels in the proper range.

The care giver needs to learn how to use alternative ways of cooking that are healthy for the client/patient. If it is possible, try to work with the client's/patient's dietician. Try to get some training on cooking diabetic meals. There are a lot of books and videos on the market, and on the internet that you can investigate to learn more about cooking diabetic meals. Find or get some books on the diet for the diabetic from the city library. Talk with your client/patient about what kinds of foods that he/she would like to eat. Try to make a weekly menu, of each day's meals, to prepare for the client/patient.

Be creative and colorful with the food you prepare for your client/patient. The more food colors you have the healthier the diet is. Try to avoid anything that has sugar.

Some foods to be careful of when you cook for a diabetic are: starchy foods, such as corn, peas, potatoes, and complex carbohydrates. White flour products, cakes, cookies, pies, and breads. Anything that has sugar. All starch and complex carbohydrates revert into sugar. Just remember, white food equates to sugar and carbohydrates.

When you cook, try to use herbs and spices. Aromatic spices are wonderful to cook with and they make the food taste so good. You can use fresh herbs or dry herbs, when you are cooking. Be careful when you use salt. Too much salt is not good for the body, especially the heart. Salt can cause hypertension, (high blood pressure). There are substitute herbs that you can use in place of using salt. You can replace salt with celery seed. It is tasty, and is great to use in recipes.

Exercise is excellent for the client/patient to do every day. Dancing while listening to good tunes on the phonograph is so much fun. When you dance, you forget all of your problems for a while. Walking is the easiest exercise anyone can do. Start walking a little each day, and increase the distance of the walk each week. Walking helps the client/patient feel better and also makes the body stronger.

Exercise is also good for you, the care giver. You need to keep yourself moving because as a care giver, you may sit a lot. Sitting too much causes you to feel tired, achy and irritable, and you gain weight. This happens to a lot of care givers. When you are in the room that you are staying in, while you are taking care of your client/patient, try to do some exercises. You need to keep active for your own well-being.

HOW TO TAKE A GLUCOSE TEST

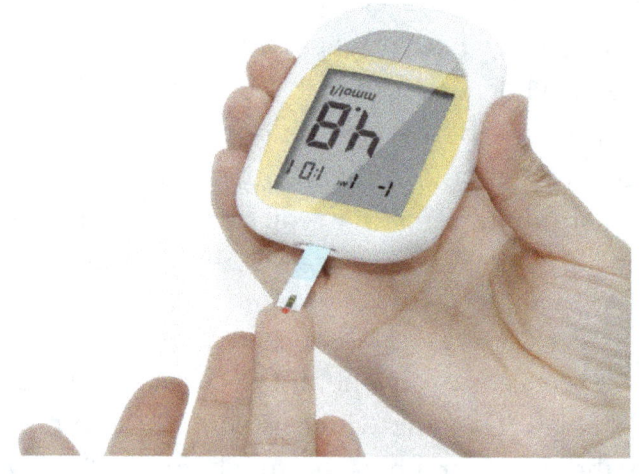

Glucose Monitor for Blood Sugar

There are many different types of Glucose

Monitors for measuring the blood sugar levels. This type of glucose monitor is the most common one to use.

Most of the time the client/patient can take his/her own blood glucose test, while using the blood glucose monitor. If you have to do the blood glucose test for the client/patient, here are the instructions.

Have the client/patient put his/her arm on the table. Take a cotton ball and put alcohol on it to clean the tip of the finger. Put the testing strip into the monitor slot. Prick the finger with the lancelet, let the blood drip onto the testing strip, (as the illustration shows). The monitor will show the numbers of the sugar glucose levels. Record this in the document journal. Put the time and the recording number.

CHAPTER 7

Grief

*May Your kindness, Lord,
be upon us; we have put
our hope in You.
Psalm 33:22 kjv.*

This picture is called Balance.
By Diana Davis

The dictionary meaning of Grief has many words, such as: grieving, sorrow, sadness, heartbreak, heartache, misery, agony, woe, suffer, anguish, distress, despondency, despair, desolation, tribulation, morn, weeping, crying, pain, grievous, tragic, agonizing, distressing, and depression.

What causes Grief? Basically, some kind of tremendous loss. This can be many kinds of losses. Grief is an emotional and physical distress, caused by a terrible tragedy, of loss. A death of a loved one, is the biggest grief inducer. There are many symptoms of Grief. Just read the "dictionary meaning of Grief."

Since the year 2001, the people in America have suffered many heavy, tragic losses. On September 11, 2001, America saw a massive murder from a group of several suicide bombers that hijacked three American commercial planes, and the suicide bombers flew to New York City, USA. These hijackers flew one of the commercial planes into the World Trade Center Towers and killed thousands of people. The World Trade Center building was totally destroyed and burned clear to the ground. Many people from all over the world worked at the World Trade Center. The tragic death toll made the word have such awful grief because of the horror of this tragic incident that happened. It wasn't just at New York City, but this same group did the same thing in two other cities and states in the United States of America on the same day, September 11, 2001.

Since the year 2001, the world has suffered many incidences from radical groups of people that committed suicide, killing people, and causing such awful trouble and horror in many countries of the world.

Many people have suffered in different ways and for different reasons. Through the loss of parents, family, children, grandparents, and friends. Loss of a home, health, and jobs. Loss of pets of all kinds. Wars and conflicts. Relationship betrayals, and divorces.

Grief has no boundaries and limits. Every person has suffered a form of grief in his/her lifetime.

Grief is hard to get over. Even years later after a tragic thing happens, the feeling of grief still comes, when you least are prepared, to deal with it. Grief affects all ages of people. Even animals have feelings of grief.

What can we do to ease the painful emotion of Grief?

When you care give a client/patient that is suffering with grief, you the care giver are a companion, and a support for your client/patient. This is a job of compassion.

Many care givers go into the homes of clients/patients, and find that there is suffering of grief that is occurring. "How can I help you? Please talk to me." The care giver asked the client/patient. Talking and listening is helpful for your client/patient. It just takes time to get over grief. Be kind and compassionate to the client/patient. Eventually the client/patient will calm down. Sometimes things will bring up your own griefs. You will feel like crying and feeling mournful. This is ok because you, the care giver, are feeling and experiencing along with the client/patient.

It takes years to get over grief. It takes a lot of counseling with a reputable doctor, counselor, or a psychiatrist. It takes the chance to forgive the past. This can help you heal from this emotion of grief. You just have to release and let go of the past. That's hard to do.

CHAPTER 8

Heart Attack

*The Lord is good,
A stronghold in the day of trouble.
Nahum 1:7 kjv.*

This is what the heart of a human really looks like.

A heart attack means the death of the heart muscle, that is caused by the reduced blood supply and oxygen to the heart. This can be caused from an obstruction in the coronary arteries, that supply the heart. The heart needs the blood, and the oxygen to keep the heart functioning.

A heart attack can happen to anyone at any age. There are many things that can contribute to a heart attack, such as age, stress, and a family history of heart disease, as well as health issues, like high blood pressure, high cholesterol, obesity. Drugs, and medicines, life changes due to hormonal changes, and the kinds of foods we eat. The way we think about ourselves, and the lifestyle we live, will also factor in how healthy our heart is.

If you have a client/patient who just arrived home from the hospital, after having a heart attack, and most likely had heart surgery. The client/patient will have a hospital release form that have all the instructions on the form. There will be the doctor's order of a list of things that the client/patient is supposed to do. There will be a list of medications that the client/patient must take at the prescribed times and the prescribed amounts.

The client/patient will have many worries and anxieties, and he/she will be in pain because of the surgery. You will have to be prepared to calm the client/patient, and reassure him/her that he/she is safe and have the best care possible. You will have to be calm too; because you will have a lot of work to do in taking care of your client/patient.

Try to find out if you can be at the client's/patient's home before he/she arrives from the hospital. Have the bed made up with fresh clean sheets, and ready for the client/patient to get into the bed, after he/she arrives home from the hospital. The client/patient will most likely be very tired and he/she will sleep for a while.

Make sure the floor is free of any obstacles, such as throw rugs, that can get in the way of the wheelchair, or the feet of the client/patient. To avoid any kind of fall or accidents, immediately remove the throw rugs.

Try to familiarize yourself with the client's/patient's home. Take the time to check where everything is located, to avoid frustration over trying to find the things you need later in the day. This can be a time-consuming aggravation, if you need something quickly.

Be a good listener, when your client/patient is talking to you. He/she will want to talk, and air out his/her feelings. He/she needs to feel comfortable and safe, as he/she will tell you what is bothering him/her. When the client/patient is talking, make sure you have eye contact with him/her. When you talk to a client/patient, talk clearly to him/her. Ask if he/she can hear you speak to him/her. Many times, people have hearing problems, and you, the care giver, want to be understood, as well as the client/patient can understand what you are saying to him/her. You have to talk clearly, and sometimes loudly, when people have hard-of-hearing, or deafness. Also make sure that the client/patient wears his/hers hearing aids. If not, remind him/her. To let people know that you are listening to them, just nod your head, or respond as he/she is speaking. This is curtesy, respectful, and mannerly.

Many care givers forget to turn off the cell phone, while he/she is working with a client/patient. This can be very irritating to your client/patient because he/she feels like you are ignoring him/her. An emergency is ok to use the cell phone, but it is very inconsiderate and rude to be using it while you are working. Cell phones can take up a lot of time, and you're not paying attention to your client, and you can forget to be aware that you have a client/patient listening in on your private conversation. This can be very embarrassing when you are confronted by your client/patient.

Monitoring the client's/patient's vital information is important. This information needs to be recorded in the documentation journal. Most of the information will be taken in the morning, after the client wakes up. There are certain times that the blood pressure will have to be taken, and the medication given. Sometimes you may have to take the blood pressure readings several times a day. You may have many telephone calls coming in from the doctor's nurses, requesting information to give to the doctor. If you need help taking a blood pressure, ask the visiting nurses. They will show you how to do the blood pressure. If the client/patient is on hospice care, there will be visiting frequent home nurse visits. The visiting nurses are a great source of help for you to learn from so that you can do a better job as a care giver.

The client/patient may have to have physical therapy. This will help the client/patient heal faster, and regain his/her strength. The therapist is a trained specialist on the exercises that the client/patient may need. The physical therapist works with the client/patient, teaching what exercises will be the best for the client's/patient's need. You the care giver will be helping your client/patient with the exercises at his/her home, on the days when there will not be physical therapy appointments. Be sure you get the list of the exercises from the physical therapist, so that you can assist the client/patient with his/her exercises.

Most likely the client/patient will want to take a nap and rest for a while. You should try to take short breaks in between the times when the client/patient is resting or taking a nap. This will help you relax and get recharged to continue the rest of your day.

When your client/patient is strong enough, try to get him/her outside so that he/she can have fresh air, and a little sunshine on his/her back and shoulder. The heat of the sun is very soothing for the muscles, and also for the bones. Just being outside feels good to the client/patient and also to you.

HOW TO TAKE A BLOOD PRESSURE

The blood pressure is measured by a monitor using two different numbers. The first number, (the top number or the highest number), is called the systolic. This tells what the pressure is in your arteries when your heart beats. The second number is the lower number, (the bottom number or the lowest number), is called diastolic blood pressure measure. This tells what the pressure is in your arteries when your heart rests between the beats of the heart.

This is the cuff blood pressure monitor.

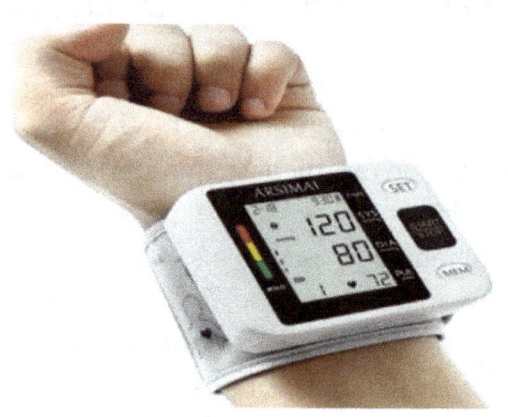

This is the wrist blood pressure monitor.

To take a blood pressure with the cuff monitor. Have the client/patient rest his/her arm on the table and relax. Make sure that the feet of the client/patient are uncrossed. You will have to put the cuff on the upper arm above the elbow. Make sure that you position the sensor directly on the inner elbow vain. Press the start button. Wait until the monitor is finished recording the blood pressure. Take off the cuff from the arm and record the readings in the documentation journal.

Take a blood pressure with the wrist monitor. Have the client/patient sit at the table, place his/her left hand on the table. Place the wrist band cuff on the wrist while making sure the sensor is on the inner wrist artery. Close the wrist band. Make sure the client's/patient's feet are uncrossed. Have the client/patient bring his/her hand up to his/her chest. Tell him/her to relax and don't move. Press the start button. Wait until the monitor is finished recording the blood pressure. Take off the wrist cuff from the wrist and record the readings in the documentation journal.

CHAPTER 9

PARKINSON'S DISEASE

*I pray to you, Lord for the time of
Your favor. God, in Your great kindness
Answer me with Your constant help.
Psalm 69:14*

Parkinson's disease is a disorder of the neurological system, usually in older adults. This is characterized by a gradual progressive muscle weakness and rigidness. It is a neurological disease that interferes with the body's chemicals that controls movement and mood.

The symptoms start mild and progress slowly to more advanced symptoms. The client will suffer a lot of depression and anxiety.

Some of the symptoms include tremors or shaking in the extremities such as the arms, hands, head, legs, and feet. Handwriting changes occur as the Parkinson's disease advances. The sleep cycle changes and sometimes there is so much restlessness because of the shaking of the body. The muscles become weak and ridged. Walking becomes more difficult to move the legs. There are a lot of digestive issues, and the stomach gets upset with different kinds of foods. The client/patient never knows when he/she will be throwing up the food he/she eats. The voice changes and it becomes hard to speak because the mouth can't form the shape of the lips to say the words properly. The volume of the voice gets softer. Dizziness is a regular occurrence and happens when the client/patient least expects it. The loss of balance is common, and the client/patient will fall easily. I would suggest that you should use a gait-belt on the client/patient so that he/she can stay steady on his/her feet. Try to never lift and walk the client/patient because you will end up using all of your strength to trying to hold up the client/patient. This will cause you to injure yourself. If all else fail, use the wheelchair. Protection is the number one priority you must think about for yourself.

People with Parkinson's disease have a high fall risk because of the uncontrolled muscle movement and also the weakness of the muscles. The client/patient shuffle then he/she walks, and his/her feet may get caught on the nap of the carpet, or he/she will accidentally catch his/her feet on items on the floor. You, the care giver, must remember there can't be anything on the floor that will trip the client. The things that should be taken off the floor, throw rugs, rubber mats, papers, toys or objects that can make the client/patient slip and fall. Rugs and carpets are very hard to push a wheelchair on. Linoleum flooring, tile flooring, and wood floors are the best to have. These floorings are safer for a wheelchair or a walker to roll easier.

Make sure the client is using a walker while walking. Sometimes you the care giver may have to help the client/patient with his/her walker to keep it moving straight. It is important that the client feels secure walking, without the fear of falling and injuring himself/herself.

When the client/patient is sitting, be sure he/she is sitting up straight. Clients/patients with Parkinson's disease have a tendency to be stooped in the chair when he/she sit. When the client/patient stands up, he/she may have a tendency to stoop, (to bend forward while standing and sitting). If the client/patient is stooping sideways, try putting a throw pillow on the leaning side of the client/patient, between the wheel chair armrest and his/her hip. If the client/patient is stooping forward, put a belt around the client's/patient's waist and around the kitchen chair or wheelchair, to keep him/her from slipping out of the chair, (a gait-belt will work just as good as a regular belt). When the client/patient is sitting in a wheelchair, you can raise the feet rest up to help lift the knees, to keep the client/patient from slipping out of the wheelchair.

When you are talking to the client/patient, sit close to him/her so that you can hear what he/she is saying to you. The client/patient may have a difficult time speaking clearly and audibly. Be patient with your client/patient. It may take a while for him/her to say what he/she wants to say. The voice might be soft spoken and hard to understand. Sometimes, clients/patients can write what he/she is trying to say. The writing may be hard to read, but you will understand what the client/patient are conveying to you.

When the client/patient is eating at the table, there are a few things that will help you while feeding the client/patient.

1. Have the client sit close to the table.
2. Put on a bib. The best kind of bib is the one that wraps around the back of the neck with a Velcro closure. Be sure you smooth the bib out and keep the bottom of the bib on the top edge of the table. This will catch the food that falls off the fork or spoon, or the liquids that spill from the drinking cup.

People with Parkinson's disease have a difficult time holding utensils and cups. The hands and fingers may have advance symptoms of the Parkinson's disease. There will be weakness, and clumsiness of the hands and fingers. Many times, the hands are shaking a lot. When the client has stress, he/she will shake more. You may have to feed your client/patient. At first, the client/patient may feel that he/she can eat his/her food by himself/herself. This is ok. If you see that the client/patient is having a challenging time eating because he/she can't control his/her hand movements, then you can ask, "Do you want me to help you?" If he/she says yes. Go ahead and feed him/her.

Foods that you can give to your client/patient should be foods that can be eaten easily. Make soft foods that can be put into a sandwich or a burrito shell. Put a paper towel around the burrito or sandwich so that the filling inside the sandwich or the burrito will not fall out onto the client's/patient's clothes.

Cook vegetables until they are soft. Fresh fruit, and also fruit juices will help relieve constipation. Prunes or prune juice is great to help relieve constipation. Make shakes that are tasty and good, this is another way for a client/patient to have nutritional food. Find out if the client/patient has a diet criterion to follow. Talk to the doctor's nurse if the client/patient has a nutritionist to help him/her with his/her nutritional guidance.

Many clients/patients with Parkinson's disease have incontinence. He/she will also experience constipation, because the muscles are affected by nerve damage from Parkinson's disease. This causes a lot of embarrassment, and clients/patients feel self-conscious. Many times, a client/patient will not tell you that he/she needs help or needs to have a diaper changed. The best thing you can do is to check the client at certain time intervals. Ask the client/patient if he/she needs to be changed, or to use the toilet. You may have to help the client/patient onto the toilet. If the client/patient can walk with a walker, let him/her. Make the job easy on yourself. Try to avoid lifting and moving the client/patient. This is very tiring to you, and it takes a lot of muscle strength to handle the client/patient that has Parkinson's disease. Lifting a client/patient can be dangerous, as there is a high risk of hurting yourself, especially your back. If you have to lift a lot, I would suggest that you use a back brace to support your back. Always have a back brace handy when you are care giving clients and patients. Always remember to take care of yourself first. If you hurt and injured yourself, you can't work.

When the client/patient is finished going to the bathroom, you will have to wipe the client's/patient's private parts, including the rectum/anus, with some toilet tissues. After you are through wiping the private parts and the rectum/anus, use a clean moist wipe. This helps the client/patient feel cleaner and more comfortable.

Put on a clean diaper or a pull-up diaper. Put a clean chuck, (moisture barrier pad to hold any fluids), on the wheel chair seat, so that the wheelchair seat doesn't get wet. This saves a lot of cleanup messes.

Try to think of ways to help yourself from working so hard, or feeling so frustrated because there is a lot to think about and work the many things you have to do as a care giver. Just be patient with yourself. Remember you are learning, and the client/patient is learning too.

LIFTING YOUR CLIENT/PATIENT

When you lift a client, use your legs. Your legs have a lot of strength than your arms and back. Bend your knees, your knees are like springs that help lift along with your legs. Don't bend yourself over the client/patient. This is a bad body movement that will hurt your back. Always try to keep your back straight. You may need to use a gait belt for assisting your client while lifting and walking him/her.

Wrap your arms under the client's/patient's armpits, and around the client's/patient's back, while you are bending your knees, and lifting the client/patient with your legs. If the client/patient can stand up on his/her own, let him/her stand on his/her own. Remember to save your back and energy.

Clients/patients have a tendency to wrap his/her arms around the care giver's neck. No, no. This is dangerous for you, and you will end up with a sore neck, and a bad headache. Always have the client/patent put his/her hands on your shoulders.

If the client/patient can stand up and move his/her feet, have the client move his/her feet along with your feet, (like a dancing couple moving together); as you turn to the right or left, have the client/patient turn with you. Try to get the client's/patient's hips and back of his/her legs aligned against the toilet seat, bed or and chair seat. Then have the client/patient sit down.

This is the process of lifting and moving a client/patient, for all or most of the lifting and moving process.

Lifting illustration

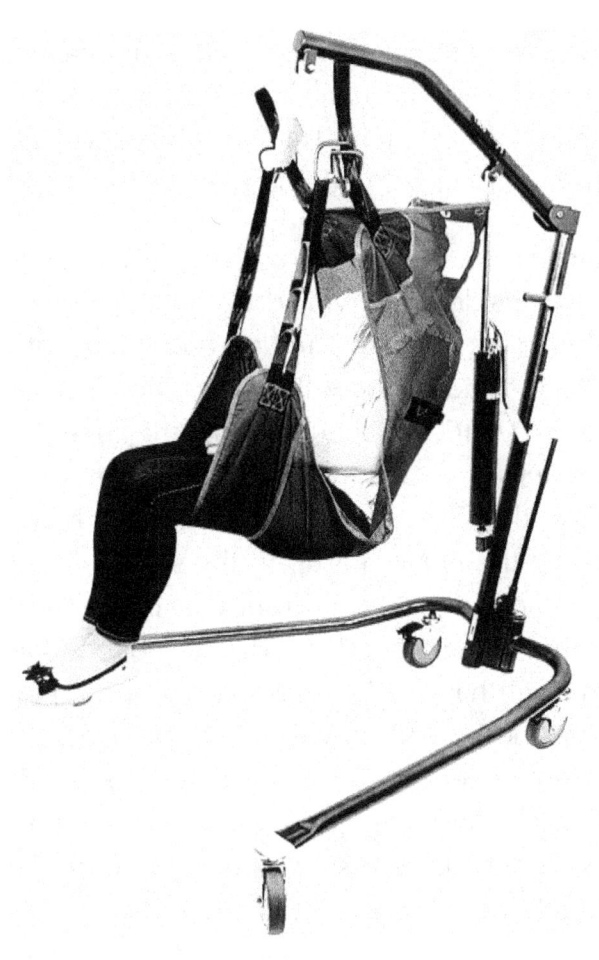

Hoyer Lift with the sling

If a client/patient is extremely heavy, tall, and/or weak, I would suggest that you use a Hoyer Lift. This is an apparatus that helps to transfer the client/patient from one place to another place, such as a bed to a wheelchair. Wheelchair to the toilet. Wheelchair to the couch.

A Hoyer Lift has a lift-bar with four chains that attach to the four corners of the seat-pad, that goes under the client/patient. Then the chains will attach to the Hoyer Lift bar with the four corner rings.

1. First you have to turn the client/patient to his/her side while lying down on the bed. Place the Hoyer-lift-sling under the client/patient. Place the Hoyer-lift-sling between the client's/patient's shoulders and the knees under the legs.
2. Turn the Client back on to his/her back.
3. Bring the Hoyer lift up to the side of the bed. Spread the Hoyer lift front part of the feet-bar with the caster-rollers. The feet of the Hoyer Lift will have to be adjusted under the bed so that the Hoyer Lift will not tip and cause the client/patient to fall. Adjust the Hoyer Lift so that the lift-bar is just over the Client/patient. Lower the lift-bar slowly until the four chains touch the mattress on top of the bed.
4. Connect the chains on each of the four corners of the Hoyer-lift-sling. Make sure the connection is secured, and the client/patient is in the correct position of the seat-pad. Have the client/patient place his/her hands on the two front chains, where it is comfortable for him/her.
5. Walk to the back of the Hoyer Lift. Find the handle bar that is attached to the hydraulic

lifting part of the Hoyer Lift. Pump the bar up and down to, (lower or lift), the lift-bar. Lift the client/patient off the bed. Check and make sure the client/patient are secure before moving the Hoyer Lift.
6. Place the wheelchair next to the bed so that you don't have to move the Hoyer lift too far away from the bed.
7. Slowly pull the Hoyer Lift away from the bed. Turn the Hoyer Lift so that the client/patient is over the wheelchair seat. Slowly lower the client/patient down into the wheelchair seat.
8. Detach the chains from the Hoyer-lift-sling. Move the Hoyer Lift away from the wheelchair. Check that the client/patient is comfortable.
9. Always keep the Hoyer-lift-sling under the client/patient. The reason for this is so that if you need to lift and move your client, he/she is already to be transferred when needed.

Clients/patient that have Parkinson's Disease have to take medications in a timely manner. It is essential that he/she take his/her medication at the same time each day. It is important that there is a medication box that is divided into different days. Each day may be subdivided into morning time, afternoon times, and night times to take the medications. Make sure clients/patients drink plenty of water while taking his/her medications. When you give clients his/her medications, use a shot-size cup or a plastic cup to serve the medications in. It is so much easier for the client/patient to put the medications into his/her mouth. If the client/patient can't hold the cup to put the medications into his/her mouth, then you will have to put the medicine into his/her mouth. Then give the water to him/her. Make sure the client/patient drinks plenty of water to swallow the pills.

CHAPTER 10

Stroke

*O Lord, my God, I cried out to
You, and You healed me.
Psalm 30:3*

By Diana Davis

A stroke, is a decrease of the blood supply to the brain. The brain is damaged if it does not get enough blood supply to keep it functioning. A stroke is also called an infraction. This affects the central nervous system, and the muscular, and skeletal system. Because of a stroke, clients/patients are disabled in his/her muscles, extremities, and also his/her speech. If the stroke hits the right side of the brain, the left side of the body will be affected. If the stroke hits the left side of the brain, the right side of the body will be affected. The client/patient can experience weakness in his/her body movements. The movements in the client's/patient's extremities are hindered too. One side of the body will not move, or it will have very little movement. The hands on either side that the stroke affects will pull up towards the wrist. The fingers will curl into the palm. The lower part of the arm will pull up, and the hand will touch the upper part of the chest. The leg will have stiffness at the joints and knees, and there will also be weakness in the muscles. The foot will drop, and the toes will point down. This is the classical happening after a stroke. The brain will have memory loss, and the stroke will affect the long-term memory, and also the short-term memory. There will be paralyses in parts of the body. The face will show the changes occurring, while the stroke is in process. The mouth will drop down, and the smile will be lopsided. The client/patient will feel dizzy and confused before a stroke. Sometimes there will be mini-strokes, before the major large stroke hits. The client/patient will pass out and go into a coma. Or there might be a heart attack occurring, during the stroke, and it will hit simultaneously.

Strokes can also cause blindness in one or both eyes. Strokes can also cause a disturbance in the client's/patient's sense of balance. Vertigo is another name for dizziness. Vertigo occurs when a client/patient has a stroke. He/she will lose consciousness, and pass out, and will be in a coma for a short time, or a long time. As the stroke is happening to the client/patient, there will be tremors, the head shaking, and the client/patient is in a slowdown response, and the nerves will show damage, as the stroke proceeds. The brain cells are dying because of the stroke. If the client/patient was a smoker, the doctors will order an aspirator, to be used to clean up the lungs. There is a tube that goes down the wind pipe into the lungs, and clears out the nicotine tar, out of the lungs. The phlegm then goes into a glass bottle. The liquids in the bottle are blackened phlegm, (a thick mucus taken out of the lungs). The nurses will change the bottle several times before there is clear liquid from the lungs, that's flowing to the bottle. I actually saw this done to my mother, when she had a massive, bleeding stroke, at the back of her head. I saw it all. Her stroke was strictly caused from smoking cigarettes.

THE SYMPTOMS OF A STROKE

The symptoms of a stroke are many. The symptoms can be so subtle that you don't know if the client/patient is having a stroke. These strokes are called, "mini," strokes. If you think your client/patient could be having a stroke, it is important to recognize the symptoms of a stroke.

- The speech may be slurred, with inability to talk.
- The tongue might look crooked, or turned to one side.
- The face may have numbness on one side.
- A part of the body may not move.
- The client/patient may not be able to walk.
- The client/patient may have a sudden heaviness in an arm or a leg.
- The client/patient may feel a tingling sensation or numbness in the arm, leg, or the face.
- The client/patient may lose control of his/her muscles.
- The client/patient will feel confused.
- The client/patient will have a headache.
- The client/patient will have vision disturbances.

- The client/patient will have dizziness, vertigo.
- The client/patient will have the loss of his/her bowels, (poop in his/her pants), and/or the loss of his/her bladder control. (pee his/her pants).
- The client/patient will throw up his/her food.
- The client's/patient's head shakes right to left, or up and down fast or slow.
- The client's/patient's mouth will drop to one side, and drool will drop off the lip.
- The client's/patient's face, on one side, will be expressionless.

The care giver must be alert about how the client/patient is feeling. Be very aware of the body responses, and movements when the client/patient is moving around. If the client/patient has a headache, take the time to check your client/patient. Talk to him/her and ask him/her how they are feeling, if he/she is in pain. If in doubt call the doctor's nurse immediately. Call for the ambulance.

When the client/patient comes home from the hospital, or the recovery center, he/she will be bringing home with him/her the medications, and the instructions from the doctor. He/she will have a diet requirement for certain foods that will be provided from the dietician's list of foods the client/patient can eat. Thoroughly read through all of the papers, and instructions. If you have any questions or concerns call the doctor's nurse.

Your client/patient may require a hospital bed for a time, while he/she is still recovering from the stroke. Room will have to be made for the hospital bed. Be sure there is plenty of room for the bed to fit in the room. Many people will have to use the living room, to accommodate the hospital bed. Be sure that the area around the room is clear of all clutter, and any fall-risk objects. This is important for your safety too. Make sure there is plenty of room to walk, and work around the hospital bed, when there is cleaning and changing for your client/patient. Make sure there is a table by the bed, to put things on it, and so that you can use it while taking care of your client/patient. Have a bed-pan available for the client/patient to use while he/she is going to the bathroom. You will have to have the client/patient lift his/her hips up high enough, to slide the bed-pan underneath his/her buttocks. Let the client/patient lower his/her buttocks onto the bed-pan. Let the client/patient lay on the bed-pan for a while, until he/she is through urinating, and having a bowl movement. When he/she is done, use toilet tissue to wipe the urine off the privates, and use more toilet tissue to wipe the stool off the anus, and the buttocks. Use a moist wipe to clean both the front and the back of the client's/patient's privates and buttocks. Have the client/patient lift his/her hips up high enough so that you can slip out the bed-pan from underneath the his/her buttocks. Pull out the dirty chuck, and put a clean chuck underneath the client's/patient's lower back and the upper legs. This will keep the bed clean and dry.

Keep Kleenex, toilet paper, and moist wipes near the client/patient so that he/she can use it for when he/she needs to blow his/her nose or wipe his/her face.

Have a bed table that can move up and down, and the feet of the table can move underneath the bed. This is really handy when the client/patient wants to read or to eat. This table is great for when you need to do a bed bath for the client/patient.

When you make meals for your client/patient, be sure to check if the prescribed diet allows green foods, such as lettuce and vegetables. Many doctors will not allow green vegetables because of the high vitamin K content. Vitamin K can make the blood coagulate too much. Many people after a stroke will be taking blood-thinning medications, to prevent the client/patient from having another stroke, from his/her blood getting too thick, and causing a blood clot, in the arteries or the veins.

Swallowing liquids can be a challenging thing for the client/patient, who has experienced a stroke. He/she is challenged on getting the mouth to close to suck on a straw, or drinking from a cup. Liquids, if it is too runny can cause the client/patient to chock and cough a lot. To remedy this problem of chocking, add a thickening agent, like instant potatoes. Mix about a teaspoon or so to thicken the water, juice, or other liquid beverages. You can buy thickeners from grocery stores, in the pharmacy area, or ask an employee that works at the store to help you find the thickener. You might check on the internet to find a liquid thickener for beverages. You may have to spoon feed your client/patient, if he/she can't feed himself/herself.

Prepare simple, soft foods for your client/patient. Using a blender is really fast and simple. Many ingredients can be added to the blender bowl. Try to make the food look appetizing and appealing. The client's/patient's appetite may be almost nonexistent. Try to convince him/her to eat. Sucking on a straw is easy for the client/patient to do, and the straw sucking strengthens his/her mouth muscles, and it helps him/her to get nutrition in his/her stomach. Keep it simple when preparing a meal. Less is better.

Get an adult bib. Put the bib on the client/patient before he/she eats. This will help tremendously in keeping the client's/patient's clothes clean. Have a moist washcloth available, to clean the client's/patient's face and hands.

If the client/patient can feed himself/herself, let him/her. He/she will feel better just knowing that he/she will have more self-control, and the abilities of taking care of himself/herself.

When you dress a client/patient that had a stroke, always remember to start dressing him/her on the weak side first. For example: when you put on a shirt, start with the weak arm first. Put the sleeve of the shirt on first. Pull the sleeve up to the shoulder, and pull up to the top of the arm. Then put the other sleeve on the other arm. Smooth out the shirt on the front and the back. If the shirt has a button closure, start buttoning from the top to the bottom of the shirt.

Be careful how you handle the client/patient when you are working with him/her. The body is sore and sensitive. Many stroke patients are very sensitive to pressure. The skin is sensitive, and it can also bruise easily. If you have to handle a client/patient be gentile, do it with a, "palm up" handling when moving the arms, and the legs. For example: When you lift the arm, reach under the arm, with the palm of your hand facing against the bottom part of the arm. The same is done for the leg.

If the client/patient uses a cane, be sure that he/she is using the cane. Many clients/patients don't like the fact that he/she have to use the cane, walker, or the wheelchair. Try to convince the client/patient that it is for his/her better health, and also to keep him/her from falling and hurting himself/herself. Be vigilant about this. Many falls can be prevented this way. Be sure to use a gait-belt whenever you move the client/patient. Remember the client/patient is weak from a stroke, and his/her balance is not stable.

Make sure that the client/patient wears supportive rubber-soled shoes. This will help in keeping his/her balance, and be steady on his/her feet. Do not let the client/patient ware house slippers that are floppy and loose. They slip off their feet, and all of a sudden there is chaos trying to balance the client/patient back onto his/her feet. Slippers don't support the feet, and they can cause a slip and fall. The client/patient can get badly injured. You don't want to try to lift a client/patient off the floor, especially if he/she weighs over two-hundred pounds or more. Remember you are not, "Super Man, or Wonder Woman." Call the fire department, to get the fire men to come, to help get the client/patient off the floor. The fire men can also help get the client/patient off the toilet, if he/she is afraid to stand up. The fire men are very nice and courteous to do this.

Have the client/patient wear a gait-belt. This belt allows you to keep control of your clients/patient, so that he/she will not lose his/her balance, while walking or moving around the house and outdoors. If outdoors, always watch out for cracked sidewalks, and uneven sidewalks, also tree roots that have roots that are rising out of the ground. The gait-belt will help you with other assisting movements, such as transferring the client/patient from a wheelchair to a couch, to a bed, toilet, bathtub, and also into a vehicle. If you are driving a truck, be careful that the client/patient doesn't lose his/her balance and fall over backwards onto yourself. Also, client's/patient's legs get bang up and gouge on his/her shins and legs. There is serious danger, with high profile vehicles such as trucks, jeeps, even semi-trucks. The client/patient can get injured, getting into the truck, and getting out of a truck. If the client/patient does get hurt, check the injury and see if the client/patient needs to have stitches. If not, do wound care on the client/patient. To do the wound care, have the client/patient sit by a table. Get a bottle of wound care cleansing solution, and a large cotton pad or sterilized gauze pad, and put the cleansing solution on the cotton pad or the sterilized gauze pad. You may have to do this a couple of times. Clean any blood around the leg. Get a sheet of paper-towel and gently dry the area that is damp. Put on antibacterial ointment onto the wound area. Cover with a band aid, or a gauze pad with bandage tape.

Before you lift a client/patient, be sure to find out if he/she can stand up by himself/herself unassisted. This saves you from lifting your client/patient. To lift a client/patient from a sitting position on a bed, couch, or other surface, place the wheelchair next to the client/patient. Lock the brakes, and make sure the tires don't move. Remove the feet-rest to the side of the wheelchair, out of the way of the client/patient, to keep him/her from bumping his/her legs and feet against the feet-rest. Stand in front of the client/patient. Place your feet on each side of the client's/patient's feet. Keep your shoulders square to your feet, and don't bend your back. Bend your knees when lifting a client/patient. Reach under the client's/patient's armpits and help him/her stand up. You may have to reach around the client's/patient's back, and lock your hands together, to lift him/her up to stand up onto his/her feet. Think of this as the client's/patient's hug. Now if the client/patient can stand up on his/her own, let him/her stand up on his/her own. Always ask first if the client/patient can stand on his/her feet on his/her own.

Once the client/patient is standing up, you both are going to walk in a semicircle, to the seat of the wheelchair, (or another chair seat). Until the back of the client's/patient's legs or hips are touching the edge of the wheelchair seat, or the edge of the chair seat. Make sure the client/patient is centered in front of the wheelchair seat, before sitting. This centered sitting goes for all seating, such as kitchen chairs, couches, recliners, and automobile seating.

If the clients/patients can sit on his/her own, let him/her do it. Otherwise, gently release your hold around the back, and under the client's/patient's armpits. Bend your knees a little to lower the client/patient to sit on the chair surface.

Just remember to keep it simple and keep the distance from one place to another place, short distances, for lift-walk the client/patient. Do not lift-walk the client/patient far distances, this is dangerous for the both of you. Think safety thoughts, before moving people.

When you are using a wheelchair, remember to lock the brakes when the client/patient is getting out of the wheelchair, or getting into the wheelchair. Remove the footrests, so that the client/patient doesn't bump his/her legs, and feet against the footrest, while standing up or sitting down. After the client/patient is seated. Replace the footrest back onto the wheelchair. Place client's/patient's feet onto the foot rests.

If the client/patient can't sit up straight in the wheelchair, you must put a seat belt, or gate-belt on him/her, to keep him/her stabilized in the wheelchair. Some wheelchairs do come with a seat belt. Use it.

Make sure the client's/patient's arms, and elbows are resting on the armrest. Be sure that his/her elbows are not going to hit any walls, doorways or other protruding obstacles. Also, keep the client's/patient's hands away from the wheel spokes. This happens a lot and there can be injuries to the hands, and especially the fingers.

When you put a wheelchair into the trunk of the automobile, before going traveling, you have to open the trunk of the car. Check the trunk to make sure the wheelchair will fit into the trunk. Remove anything that will be in the way, of the wheelchair fitting into the trunk. Take off the footrests, place them on the side of the car trunk. Bring the wheelchair to the back of the car. Pull the straps upward to pull/close the seat of the wheelchair together. Lock the breaks to the tires. Now slowly lift the wheelchair, and let the wheelchair lean into the trunk. Adjust the wheelchair so that it will sit in the trunk, without too much movement, while the car is moving. Close the car trunk lid. Now you're off and running to have some fun. Check out the sights around the area that you are going through, while driving.

Be aware of your body movements when you are putting the wheelchair into the car trunk. Use the strength of your legs, when you are doing any kind of lifting.

Most people who have incontinence after experiencing having a stroke, he/she will lose the ability to feel the urge to go to the bathroom, to urinate and have a bowl movement. The muscles, and the nerves that control the bladder and bowels, are weakened from a stroke. The client/patient may be wearing a disposable diaper. There are many brands of deposable diapers to choose from.

To change an adult disposable diaper is very simple. Put a liquid absorbing pad, (chuck), on the bed. Have the client/patient lie onto his/her back. Pull the disposable diaper seam sides apart to open the diaper. Clean all the fesses, (poop), off the privates. Take a moist wipe and wipe off all the urine off the skin and buttocks. Pull out the dirty diaper and throw it into the trash receptacle. Put on the clean diaper. Start at the feet, put the feet into the leg holes. Gently pull up the diaper until it is pulled up to the hips, have the client/patient lift his/her hips up off the bed, you can now finish pulling the diaper to where the client/patient is comfortable. Make sure the skin is dry. Put a little baby powder on the client's/patient's privates so that he/she will feel dry and be comfortable. Put on the client's/patient's pants and shoes. Help the client/patient get back into the wheelchair.

Always respect the client's/patient's privacy and dignity. This is the most personal, and embarrassing experience that the client/patient has to endure. Always ask for his/her approval of being touched, and having to change his/her diaper, clothes, and any form of undressing, and dressing.

If the client/patient is bedbound, and can't move or turn alone, you will have to use a draw-sheet to turn, and move the client/patient. A draw-sheet is a top sheet, that is folded lengthwise, three times. Make sure the three parts are even in width and in length. (Check the illustration below). After you fold the draw-sheet, place it on the bed so that the long part is across the upper part of the bed, where the shoulders are, and down to where the knees will be. The ends of the draw-sheet should be draped on each side of the bed.

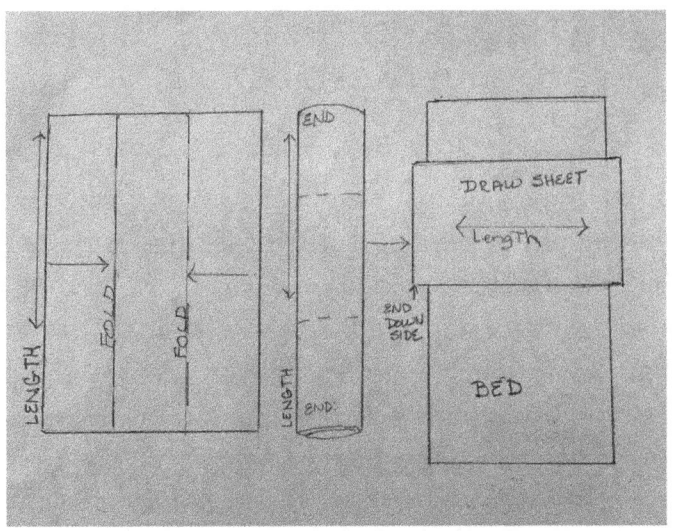

Draw sheet instructions on folding the top sheet by Diana Davis

TURNING THE CLIENT/PATINT

To turn the client/patient, you need to stand on one side of the hospital bed, or regular bed. Pick up the draw sheet ends that are on the opposite side of the bed from where you are standing, so that you can turn the client/patient towards you. Firmly take the end of the draw sheet where the folded corners will be. Gently pull the draw sheet, to make the client/patient turn towards you. Take a pillow and place it behind the client's/patient's back. This is to keep him/her from rolling backwards onto his/her back. Always remember to turn the client/patient toward you when you turn him/her because you will stop him/her from rolling off the bed.

TO MOVE THE CLIENT TOWARDS THE HEADBOARD

If the bed is a hospital bed, you will have an easier time moving the client/patient in the bed. The benefit of the bed is that it is an electric bed, that has the head at one end part of the bed, that goes up and down, and the foot end part, of the bed that goes up and down. Were the knees and hips set on the bed, this area lifts up and down. These beds are built for the greatest benefit of comfort for the client/patient, and a big benefit for the care giver to move the client/patient in different positions on the bed. The manual hospital bed will have levers and turn handles to lift and lower the bed sections. This is good too. Just a bit more work and slower to use.

To move the client/patient to the headboard of the hospital bed, you will need to raise the bottom, foot part of the bed up to the highest position. Go back to the top part of the bed, lower the headboard part of the bed to the lowest position. The reason for this is that gravity will help you easily move the client to the headboard. When you pull the client/patient, pull the draw sheet behind the client's/patient's shoulders towards the headboard, where you are standing. The draw sheet will slide easily toward you. Doing this move, will save you a lot of muscle strain from pulling the client/patient. This will save you a lot of straining, and struggling with the client/patient, while you slide the client/patient up and down the bed.

To move the client/patient towards the foot part of the bed. You will have to raise the headboard part of the bed as high as you can, then walk to the foot part of the bed and lower the foot part of the bed as much as you can. Reach up to grab the draw sheet folded ends, and pull the client/patient towards you. Level out the bed. Adjust the bed until the client/patient is comfortable.

When the client is sitting in the hospital bed make sure he/she is sitting in the hip section of the bed. Raise the head part of the bed so that the client is sitting up. Now bring up the knee by raising the knee part of the bed. Think of this as the V pocket for the hips to stay put and not shift. The client/patient will be comfortable in this position, and can sit like this to eat, watch television, read, and write.

The hospital bed can be raised up and down. This is good for when the care giver needs to work with the client/patient for the washing and changing. This will also save the care giver from straining his/her back.

If your client/patient is on oxygen, he/she will have an oxygen condenser that makes oxygen and sends the oxygen through a plastic clear tube. On the front of the oxygen condenser unit, there is a regulator knob that raises and lowers the amount of oxygen. This regulator has a silver-liquid that tells you how much oxygen is flowing. Keep the amount of oxygen to the prescription of what the doctor orders. If the oxygen is at the number 3 or higher, most likely that is too high amount of oxygen. Be sure that the correct amount is set.

The filter keeps the air clean that comes into the oxygen condenser. This filter should be replaced once a year or oftener. If you rent the oxygen condenser, call the medical supply company, and ask for a repair man to replace the oxygen condenser filter. If the filter is not changed often enough, the client/patient risks getting a sinus infection and irritations in the nose area and the sinuses. Also, the lungs can get an infection too.

Most clients/patients have to have humidity with his/her oxygen. On the back of the oxygen condenser, there is a cup, that have distilled water in it. There is a screw top lid that have a tube connected to the oxygen hose. The moisture in the cup will evaporate through the tube and provide the moisture that the client/patient needs to keep his/her nasal and sinus chambers from drying out.

The plastic clear or green tubes, that connects to the nozzle on the oxygen condenser, come in different lengths, to help reach the client/patient. Some are fifteen feet long, and will work in a small bedroom or a den. The longer tubing will be twenty-five feet long, and also there are fifty feet long tubes. It all depends on the size of the room the client/patient is staying in. Some people will walk all over his/her home with the long tube, dragging behind him/her. When the oxygen tube is not being used, try to wind it up like a yard hose, and place it in a corner or next to the oxygen condenser unit. When coiling the tube, be sure you do it loosely. If it is coiled too tightly, this could cut off the oxygen supply to the client/patient. I want to reiterate this again, "If the client/patient is walking around in the house, with the oxygen tube loose, and dragging behind him/her on the floor, make sure that the client/patient will not get the oxygen tube caught under his/her feet. This can cause a very serious injury." I had a client that had a trip/fall because she got up suddenly from her chair, and walked into her oxygen tube, she fell into a doorway. She broke her wrist. I had to do first aid on her. She banged up her head, and broke her wrist. I made a make shift splint for her wrist, by putting two wood spoons on each side of her wrist. I found some tape and wrapped it around her wrist, to stabilize the hand and wrist. She bandaged her head where she banged it against the door way. I had to take her to the hospital emergency, to get a cast put on her wrist.

I would suggest that the care giver learn about first aid. A first aid kit is handy when you get into situations that demand immediate wound care, and injuries. Be sure there is a first aid kit in the kitchen, or the bathroom, where you can find it easily. When you start working with a client/patient, check the first aid kit, to be sure there is everything you need, just in case you have an emergency.

There is another tube that can connect to the long main tube with a double ended connecter. This tube is called a cannula. This cannula has two small holes with a short thin tube that fits just inside the nostrils. This is where the oxygen comes out, and through the nostrils. The client/patent can breathe fresh oxygen. Check the cannula tube to see if it has any mucus matter that can get into the tube. If the tube looks dirty in any way, then change the cannula tube, and throw away the used cannula tube. Ideally the cannula tube should last a month or so. But if the client/patient is sick, change the cannula tube every few days.

Oxygen Tank. This tank has a monitor of the amount of oxygen that is contained inside the oxygen tank. When there is oxygen inside the tank, it will have a hissing sound because the oxygen is coming out through the nozzle, that the plastic tube is hooked to, and the oxygen will come out of the cannula tube, through the nose piece. Check the monitor frequently. Have another oxygen tank ready to change when the older oxygen tank goes empty. There will be a lever on top of the tank, to turn off and on the oxygen. Turn off the oxygen in the old tank. Pull off the plastic tubing from the nozzle. Remove the oxygen tank and put it where the medical supply truck will pick up the oxygen tank. Put the new oxygen tank by the client/patient. Place the plastic tubing onto the nozzle, and turn on the oxygen, to the number of the volume amount of oxygen output, for the client/patient to breathe.

There are a lot of things that you have learned in this chapter and to remember. Care giving takes time to learn. Just take it one day at a time. Remember, the story of the little engine: "I think I can do it; I think I can do it, I did it!"

When you feel overwhelmed, do things in smaller intervals. It takes a lot of patience and learning how to understand your client/patient. Be gentle and caring on yourself. Be loving and take care that your needs are met. When the client/patient is in bed for the night, you relax. Take a bath and soak in the tub for a short while.

Always remember, when the client takes a nap, you take a nap too. Rest when you can. Take advantage to rest when your client/patient is resting. This is my secret to lasting many years, doing care giving. I worked 24/7 weeks on end with some clients/patients. I had to survive the long working hours and days. Some days were easy. some days was awful. Some days were Hell! There are the good, the bad, and the terrible. You can do this and come out better because you are strong, and you have faith in your higher power, God, Universe, deity however you believe, that is ok. Believe in yourself.

CHAPTER 11

Surgeries

*Whatsoever ye shall ask in prayer,
Believing, ye shall receive.
Matthew 21:22 kjv.*

There is always someone to help, us in life.
The orchids grown by Diana Davis

A surgery is an operation or a treatment to remove a diseased part of the body. People have surgeries at any age. Men have surgeries, women have surgeries, children have surgeries. Technology is such that babies can have surgeries in the womb before he/she is born.

As people get older, he/she start having problems in the joints, caused by injuries, arthritis conditions, and broken bones from falls. Other people have problems with the inside organs of the body. The Lungs, heart, liver, stomach, intestines, colon, and kidneys. Surgery encompasses many parts of the body of a human being.

After a client/patient has surgery, he/she will typically spend time in the hospital recuperating in a recovery facility. This can take a week, months, or longer. It all depends how a client/patient heals.

The client/patient will be taking different kinds of medications for infection and pain. When clients/patients come home from the hospital recovery, he/she will have the doctor's release order with the instructions that the client/patient will need to adhere to. There will be a schedule for changing bandages, and when to put certain medications on the surgery site. He/she will be feeling overwhelmed and tired. Some clients/patients will be feeling weak and have no strength.

The client/patient will be taking many medications that the doctor prescribed for him/her to take. He/she may be experiencing weakness, dizzy spells, and he/she is unstable to stand. When a client/patient is in a lot of pain, he/she should rest. Pain has a way of making you feel tired. It takes a lot of energy to deal with pain. Because of all of the above problems, dizzy spells, and unable to stand, the care giver will have to stay close to the client/patient to assist him/her so that he/she will not fall. If the client/patient have a walker, make him/her use it. Safety is a priority.

The care giver will need to be prepared to assist and protect the client/patient. You will need to be sure the client/patient is obeying the doctor's orders. He/she is taking his/her medications, and having the bandages changed at certain time schedules. Sometimes the client/patient will feel so great because he/she is not in pain, because he/she is on pain medicine and the medicine will make the client/patient have too much confidence and get carless and fall. This is not good. During this time, don't leave the client/patient alone at any time. The first two days after coming home from the hospital are the most dangerous days for the client/patient to get hurt badly and end up back into the hospital.

When the client/patient goes to bed, have the bed ready before he/she is ready to go to bed. Help the client/patient change his/her clothes and put on the pajamas or a night gown. Have the client/patient brush his/her teeth and go to the bathroom before going to bed. This helps the client/patient sleep better and longer in the night.

If there is a monitor to hear the client/patient calling for you, you will be able to hear him/her. I always suggest a baby monitor. This is useful when there are noises, and movement in the client's/patient's bedroom.

Be sure you are in close proximity to the client's/patient's bedroom. You must be able to hear and see the client/patient. Make sure the client/patient is not doing anything that can cause injury. At any time of the day and the night, the client/patient might try to risk doing something on his/her own. Even try to go outside the house. During the night you may have to reassure clients that he/she are safe, and everything is ok in the house.

People hate to admit that he/she needs help, and that he/she is dependent on a care giver to help him/her. It doesn't matter what the nature of the illness is, injury, or surgery is. People fear to acknowledge that he/she needs help.

I had a client who had hip surgery. She was very determined to walk alone before she was supposed to. The woman was a very active athlete goffer and a senior citizen. In the middle of the night, she got out of her bed, (a hospital bed), walked around the house, she decided that she had to go to the bathroom. While she is the bathroom, she grabbed the towel rack and used it to be supporting herself while trying to sit on the toilet. The towel rack came loose from the wall, and she fell to the floor, screaming, and a loud crash sound. I jumped out of the bed that I was sleeping in, and ran to the bathroom that the client was in. I saw her on the floor with the towel rack still in her hand and leaning against the toilet. It was dark in the bathroom, because she didn't turn on the light for fear she would wake me up. She didn't want help. I asked her, "Why did you not call for me to help you?" Her reply was, "I wanted to do it myself." This is a classic example of how stubborn clients/patients can be.

To help clients/patients from getting bored while he/she are recovering from the surgery, and to keep him/her from having too much time to think about his/her problems. You can read books to the client/patient, that is if he/she can't see to read. Have books and magazines for the client/patient to look at and read. Play card games. Put a puzzle together, with your client/patient. Go for walks together. If the client/patient has a wheelchair, help him/her sit into the wheelchair, and go for a walk. Basically, let the client/patient do what he/she wants to do, as long as it is safe for him/her. If you are fixing meals, have your client/patient help you. They love that.

CHAPTER 12

Vertigo and Dizziness

*Give ear, Listen humbly,
For the Lord speaks.
Jeremiah 13:15 kjv.*

What is Vertigo? Another name is Dizziness. Vertigo is a common problem that happens to many people. It has no age barrier. Many things can happen to people at different times in his/her life, that can cause this disturbing unbalanced feeling. When you get Vertigo, it hits you like a ton of bricks, smacking you in the head. You have a sensation of being off-balanced. You try to get up, and all of a sudden you fall backwards onto your back. The ability to get up while whirling in your head and feeling totally incapable of moving right. The room spins around you. Vertigo feels like a raging drunk, and you can't get up from the bed, or the floor.

The time Vertigo seems to hit most people is in the morning after a night of sleep. The feeling of slight dizziness can occur days ahead before the real impact of Vertigo hits you.

What causes Vertigo? There are many reasons that causes Vertigo.

- When you wake up in the morning, from a night's sleep, you sit up quickly and all of a sudden you get dizzy, and feel like you are falling backwards, and you will fall backward onto the bed, or onto the floor.
- Getting out of bed and standing up too fast will cause you to be dizzy, and feel nauseated. Sometimes people will pass out, or faint.

- Walking and turning your head can cause you to get dizzy. You could miss-step or loose the rhythm of walking.
- Moving your head can make you dizzy.
- Bending down to tie your shoes can make you feel woozy, and the room will look like it is going in a circle around you.
- Bending down suddenly can cause you to lose your balance, and you will feel the dizziness hitting you.
- Drinking too much alcoholic beverages is a drunk that smacks a Vertigo go round in your head, and you end up with a roaring headache.
- A head injury and having a concussion can cause Vertigo.
- Going to the amusement park and riding the roller costar rides will definitely cause dizziness, and when you get off the ride, you can't walk straight for a while.
- You may have an infection in your ears called Labyrinthitis. This is an inflammation of the labyrinth. This is the fluid-filled canals and sacs in the inner ear. These canals and sacs are in the Vestibular system, that controls a person's balance, and eye movement. One or both of your ears and eyes can be

affected from Labyrinthitis.
- The ears may have ringing, this is called, Tinnitus.
- The ears might feel like they are full of something.
- Viral infections in the inner ears can cause Vertigo.
- The eyes will be twitching and going in and out of focus. This too causes the Vertigo dizziness.
- High blood pressure and/or low blood pressure.
- Extreme fatigue, and tiredness.
- Having a stroke.
- The Flu, viruses, and illnesses.

Vertigo can last for a short time, many weeks, many months or more. Many people need time for this condition to go through its course of healing. Many people will end up having to have physical therapy, and do the exercises that will help the client/patient heal from this condition.

When you have a client/patient that have Vertigo, dizziness, you will have to be close by ready to assist the client/patient. Vertigo makes the client/patient very unstable on his/her feet. The client will be moving slow when he/she is walking. The fear is high in his/her thoughts because the control to stand up and walk is a frightening feeling because the surroundings are looking like it is moving in a circle around the client/patient.

If the client/patient is going to physical therapy, stay close, watch and listen to what the physical therapist is saying and doing. The client/patient might be coming home with a list of exercises to do each day. The care giver will have to assist the client while working on the exercises.

If you have any concerns about the client/patient, don't hesitate to call the doctor office, and/or call the physical therapist office.

In the morning when the client/patient is ready to get up and move around, put a gait-belt on him/her. This will give you, a better leverage and control in assisting the client/patient.

If the client/patient is using a cane, make sure he/she are using the cane. The cane will help with the dizziness while the client/patient is walking.

Make sure your client/patient is wearing supportive shoes. Preferably lace up tennis shoes, or rubber soled shoes. No slippers or flip flops.

CHAPTER 13

VIRUS

*Faith precedes the miracle,
I am healed.
Thank you
By
Diana S, Davis*

This is a collage that I did in 2011, after I had a dream of Jesus.
(Hebrews 13:8)
Diana Davis

What is a virus? A virus is a highly infectious germ, that spreads rapidly between people, animals, and species. It is deadly. It attacks many different parts of the body.

The virus mutates frequently, and changes to be a different variant, to attack to the body. The recent virus, the covid 19, has mutated many times since the first outbreak occurred early in the year 2020. Viruses attach to the weakest parts of the body. It can change the DNA and RNA of our cells, and the virus will change the cell molecular coding of the DNA and RNA. It hits the lungs, heart, ears, stomach, the blood, and many other parts of the body.

Viruses enter through the mouth and nose. Touching the face with dirty hands. Wearing a mask will help stop most of the viruses.

The symptoms of a virus are a sore throat, aches and pains, headaches, runny nose, sneezing, coughing up discolored sputum, and a high fever, pneumonia, stomach aches, nausea, diarrhea, flu-like symptoms, fatigue, upper respiratory problems, rashes, sores blisters, and warts. The virus will usually last two to three days. After the third day the symptoms will gradually go away.

Viruses are spread through touching, sneezing, dirty surfaces, and countertops. Dirty clothing that has been exposed to the virus germs. Many facilities will have the employees wear a shield, this is a clear covering for the face, a cotton lab coat will be provided for the employee to wear so that he/she is protected. Wearing gloves will protect you from getting the virus.

The care giver who is working in an environment that has patients/clients sick with a virus, the care giver will have to be prepared to wear a mask and ware latex or plastic gloves. The mask will help protect you from getting sick with the virus. If you are at a private home, and the client/patient is sick. Put a mask on yourself, and on the client/patient. Immediately have the patient checked if the illness is a virus. Call the doctor's office to get a test done on the client/patient, for what kind of virus the client/patient has. If the client/patient has home nurses coming to the home, ask the nurses to do a test on the client/patient.

After helping, touching, washing, toilet use, changing diaper. Wash your hands. Always use a paper towel to dry your hands. Always be clean in everything you do.

When you go home, have a plastic bag in your car that is ready to put your shoes in it. Have a pair of extra shoes in your car to change into. Keep alcohol hand cleaner in your car. Use it after working, shopping, eating out in a restaurant, and going to the public bathroom.

When you get home, go to the washroom where you have your clothes washer and put your clothes in it. Put everything you have worn that day into the clothes washer. After you do this, go take a shower, and wash all your body, yes, shampoo your hair. By adhering to this regimen of cleaning and cleanliness, will assure you that your home environment is free from the contamination of the viruses.

Viruses have a tendency to grab onto the hair, clothes, and everything that is exposed to the virus in the environment. The reason is that viruses are circular shaped germs that have spikes around the outer shell, that cover the virus germ. These spikes are a way that the viruses can get attached to surfaces, up into the nasal area, into the mouth, and into the insides of the body. This is where the real harm will occur, inside of your body. Viruses mutate frequently. The mutated part are the spikes. The spikes, they change in shape and color. As the spike changes into different shapes, so is the strength of the virus germ, it gets more volatile and stronger.

It is very important that you keep the mask on at all times. Many hospitals, rest homes, and retirement homes have a higher incident of viruses and sickness. Especially with the Corona virus 19, that hit in 2020. This was and still is a deadly virus because its potency and outer surface spikes keep changing.

When you are working on the job, take care of yourself. Get lots of rest. Go to bed early, turn off the computer, and the cell phone at least an hour before you go to bed. When the client/patient is resting, you rest. Also keep your distance whenever possible.

Drink lots of liquids to keep yourself hydrated. A hydrated body will fight off sicknesses. Eat good nourishing foods, such as fruits, vegetables, soups, and warm drinks. With a virus going around, I would suggest that the food is cooked. Wear gloves when you are preparing food. When you are done, prepping and cooking. Take off the gloves and throw them away into the trash receptacle.

If you are feeling stress, and anxiety coming on, stop what you are doing and take a break. It is ok to take breaks often. Breaks give you the opportunity to sit for a spell and just clear away the worries and fears. Watch television with your client/patient. Television is a great way to forget for the moment of what is pressing to you. Put on some calming music. This will be good for you and also for your client/patient. This breaks up the routine of the day, and it is a good time to use the cell phone or your computer, for a short while. But don't forget your client/patient that he/she can hear everything you are saying. They may fake deafness, and he/she will know your private business. Always remember you are #1. Take care of yourself.

CHAPTER 14

DEATH

*Honor thy father and thy mother,
That thy days may be long upon the land.
Exodus 20:12 kjv*

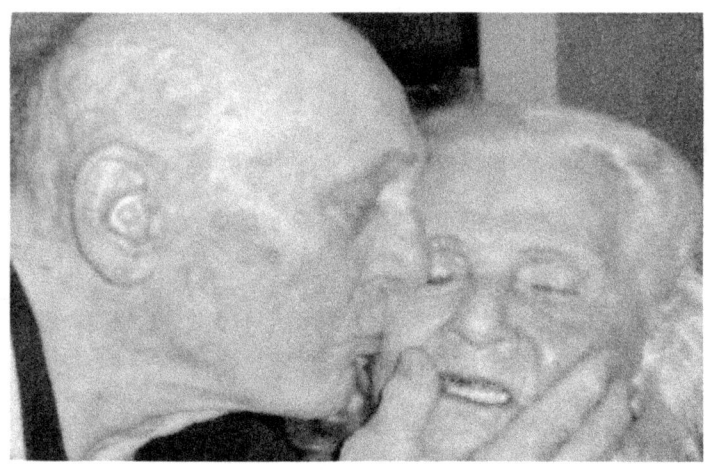

This is my mother, Esther with her husband, Virg,
Esther died at the age of 89 yrs. old,
Virg died at the age of 94 yrs. old.

Death is when the body stops functioning. The heart stops beating, and the brain ceases to function.

Death is a natural thing that happen to all of us. Some of us die young, and some of us die old.

There are no limits to death. Everything on the planet earth dies. People die, animals die, birds die, bees die, plants die, trees die, and flowers die. Every race, color, or group of people dies. Death is a natural thing.

Care givers need to learn to know about death. Care givers need to be at peace with death. We need to know what happens to the client/patient, during the dying process. The care giver will have to help the client/patient, while he/she is going through the experience of the dying process. His/her emotions and fear are at the forefront of the process of dying.

Care givers need to understand the concerns that the client/patient may have about himself/herself. The concern of what is going to happen to his/her pets. Many times, when a client/patient is dying, the client's/patient's pet will want to stay beside his/her master until the client/patient is dead. Pets have an intuitive instinct to know when the person that loves them so much, is ready to die. The pet will grieve, whimper when he/she hears the master crying, talking. Most clients/patients do have the frightening feeling of the unknown mystery, questioning himself/herself, if there is life after a person dies.

Care givers must be patient and understanding when a client/patient is dying. It can be a frightening feeling. Some care givers comment that he/she has the heebie-jeebies, or a creepy feeling. Not every care giver can be around death. It takes a lot of courage to do this kind of care giving. What helped me on my fears, and preconceived ideas about death, was, I prayed at lot, and asked God, my higher power, my guardian Angels, to help me understand death, and not to be afraid to do this kind of care giving job. A since of peace came upon me, and I felt the compassionate agape love for the client/patient.

Be reassuring and do the care that you know how to do. Stay with your client/patient. There will be friends, and family members coming, and going, to see the client/patient. Give these people time alone with his/her father, mother, grandparents, children, and other people. This is the time you can leave the room, step outside, and take a much-needed break.

You, the care giver, need to understand the different religions, and beliefs that your clients/patients have. Not every person on this planet has the same beliefs. Many families can be diversified into different belief systems, within the family. I would recommend that you study about world history, world cultures, world religions, and learn how people believe, and live his/her life. Study how different countries, use religion, and the belief system to run the country. Religion is also a cultural system, as how people live his/her life in the culture that is the predominant system. Having the knowledge of the traditions and customs of the client/patient, will help you know what to do to help your client/patient feel comfortable with you being there with him/her.

Learning about the religions, and the system of the family beliefs, also, the countries cultures, will help you understand how you can be a better servant, care giving to your client/patient.

Does the client/patient have any issues of anger, or resentment, towards anyone in the family? Have these issues been addressed with the family? What are the last wishes that the client/patient have, for the time of death?

Is there an Advance Directive Order, (ADO), that specifies what the client wants done when he/she can't take care of himself/herself and make decisions about the end-of-life decisions. Is there a DNR, (Do Not Resuscitate), document stating wither the client wants to be resuscitated if he/she starts to die, or is unconscious? These documents need to be placed where everyone, who are taking care of the client/patient sees it. Most people put this DNR document on the front of the refrigerator.

What is the power of attorney's, (this can be a family member, a friend, or another person), instructions for the care of his/her family member, friend or client/patient?

These questions are extremely important to have, and that they are understood. When you start to take care of the client/patient, you need to read and sign in on the document, that you have read all of the important documents. If there are questions and issues, please don't hesitate to ask questions. There should also be a telephone number that you can call if you need to know about something, that you are questioning about.

Clients/patients will experience a lot of feelings and emotions, while going through the process of dying. He/she may want to talk about his/her life, feelings, what he/she has done in his/her life. His/her emotions can be outbursts of crying, reminiscing, and rehashing the same thing over, and over. He/she may be angry at God for letting himself/herself have to die, at this time of his/her life. The repeat of why now? Why didn't so and so come see me before I got so sick? A lot of arguments between the family members, and the client/patient can get very distressing to the client/patient, and especially to you, the care giver. When family members, and or friends come to visit, and you feel the feeling that the room is getting negative, excuse yourself and walk out of the room. Most of the negativity is between the family. You don't need to feel that you have to stay in the same room, while there are personal, private family talks. This is giving respect to the client's/patient's privacy.

Basically, the dying process is the same for each person. Some people die peacefully, and others will have a miserable, painful death. As the body goes through the different stages of the dying process, changes happen to the body. What kind of disease or sickness the client may have, determines the process of the death changes of the body.

Some of the death stages of the body, from the beginning until death, are as follows:

1. Symptoms of the disease or illness.
2. Advancement and increase of the complications of the disease or illness.
3. Weakness in various areas of the body.
4. Having a hard time staying focused, thoughts, memories, or in anything, or anyone.
5. Increase of pain, and confusion.
6. The internal organs start to breakdown, and this will cause a lot of pain.
7. The amount of urine, and bowel movements will decrease, and eventually cease.
8. The lungs will fill up with phlegm. The client/patient will try to cough up the phlegm,

and it might get caught in the throat. This is the beginning of the death raddle. The death raddle can progressively get louder as time goes until the client passes away. When the phlegm builds up and it gets hard for the client/patient to breathe, you can use an aspirator machine to suck up the phlegm. This will help the client/patient be more comfortable.

9. The client/patient will get delirious and may start speaking to something that is either imaginative, or trying to talk to a dead relative. There are reports of dying people seeing dead people.
10. Just before the client/patient dies, he/she will become really quiet and feel at peace. The eyes will be closed or partially open. The breathing will get shallower and quieter.
11. Clients/patients will take in a deep last breath of air, close his/her eyes, and pass away. Sometimes the eyes will not close.

When clients/patients are in the process of dying, try to stay with him/her. Give a lot of comfort and love to him/her. Rub his/her forehead, and hairline. This seems to help relax the feelings of stress, and pain. The eyes may be closed, tears may be flowing, so have a tissue to wipe the tears off the face. You can talk to the client/patient. He/she can still hear you. Talk soothing things.

About two hours before the client/patient dies, give him/her a bed bath. Make sure the water is warm. Be very gentle and not to rub too much. As the skin is breaking down and will bleed or tare easily. Use a sponge. This will be gentler on the skin. Dry as you go. After the bed bath, put a clean diaper on the client/patient. This bath and a clean diaper are giving dignity to the client/patient.

Have a tee-shirt ready to put on the client/patient. Before you put the tee-shirt on the client/patient, cut the back of the tee-shirt in the center from the hem to the neck. This will make it easier to put the tee-shirt on the client/patient. Slip the tee-shirt, with the open back of the tee-shirt lying on each side to the client/patient, put the arm through the sleeves on of the tee-shirt. Put a clean chuck underneath the client/patient between the shoulders and the knees. Clients/patients may release his/her bowels and urinate as he/she is dying. Also, the chuck helps with the bleeding of the skin and absorbs the blood.

Here are some comfort measures you can do to help your client/patient, during the last week of his/her life.

The client/patient will be in a lot of pain. Stay in constant contact with the hospice doctors and nurses. They will help you with what to do for your client/patient. There will be an end-of-life packet that the hospice doctor ordered for the client. This includes the comfort medications to give to the client/patient to help him/her stay calm and free of pain. You can talk to the hospice nurses about any questions you have. Hospice will send out a nurse to check up on the client/patient. If you need some help, or have questions that need to be answered, the nurses will help you. Hospice also has clergy-Chaplains that will come out to see the client/patient. The chaplain might help you the care giver too. The chaplain will have a prayer, and scripture reading with you and the client/patient. This is very helpful at this time, for the client/patient. There is a sense of peace, just being spiritually reassured.

Every two hours, turn your client/patient to his/her side. After two hours, turn your client/patient onto his/her back. After two hours, turn your client onto the opposite side. Think of a circle as you turn your client/patient. On left side, on back, on right side, on stomach. Back on to the left side. This turning of your client/patient is to avoid having pressure sores, or bedsores. Pressure sores appear on the protruding parts of the body, such as the spine, hip bone, shoulders, arms, and legs. The buttocks are another area that can get real sore bedsores. This is because of the moisture, that accumulates in the diaper. If you see any red spots or sores anywhere on the body, make note of it and document it in the documentation journal. Put rash or bedsore ointment on the client/patient. The ointment will help to eliminate the bedsores and the rashes.

Put travel-size pillows under the heels of the feet, and to the mid-calf of the leg, to keep the skin from peeling or getting pressure sores. Place larger pillows underneath each elbow to ease strain on the arm, and from the shoulder from being pulled down by the weight of the arm. Put a large pillow under the knees. This helps ease the pain that can be in the lower back and hips. This also helps to relax the muscles.

Put flannel top sheets in the dryer to warm them up. Cover the client/patient with warm flannel top sheets. This is very soothing and warming for him/her. Clients/patients just love this. I use this on clients/patients that are not in the end stages of his/her life. I even like putting a warm flannel top sheet on me.

Be sure to use the draw-sheet under the client/patient for easy movement of the body, in the hospital bed. Clients/patients that are dying get heavy and feel like he/she has no strength. This is one of the most important reasons to use the draw-sheet. When you turn the client/patient onto his/her side, place a large pillow behind the back. This will keep the client/patient from rolling backwards. The draw-sheet also makes it easy to change the clothing and the diaper. When you turn the client/patient to his/her side, be sure to put a pillow under his/her head, to support the head so that the head is not hanging. This causes a headache, and it hurts the neck and shoulder. Put a pillow between the knees so that the client/patient doesn't get pressure sores on the bony parts of the knees, and this also helps to relax the hip joints.

Put socks on the client's/patient's feet. This helps to keep his/her feet warm, and to protect the skin on the heels of the feet from pealing and getting pressure sores.

If the client's/patient's hands are clenched into a fist, get a facecloth, small towel. Roll the facecloth or towel into a roll-shape. Try to put the rolled-up towel into the hand. Gently pull the fingers and place each finger onto the rolled facecloth or towel. Check the client's/patient's fingernails. If the fingernails are too long or are starting to scratch the client's/patient's palm, trim the nails. Use a fingernail file to smooth out the nail tip. You may have to put a sock on the hands, to keep the hands warm and also prevent the client/patient from scratching himself/herself.

When your client/patient dies, you will have to call the hospice doctor or nurse. He/she will guide you as to what to do for the client. He/she will guide you regarding the procedure, and the giving of medications that have not been used, and how to dispose of it, or the hospice may want the medication back. Hospice will send a nurse to document the time the client/patient has died. Hospice doctors will call the coroner to pick up the client/patient and take him/her to the mortuary.

If you are working for an agency, call your work agency, let the owners, supervisor, or whoever is in charge know of the death of the client/patient. Give the time that the client/patient died. The agency will call the family of the client/patient and call the power of attorney of the client/patient.

Being a care giver for a dying person is not easy. There is a lot of work in the end process of the dying client/patient. Some of the things I mentioned to do are not easy to do, and it takes a lot of courage to do them. You may feel nauseated, because of the care you had to do. Using an aspirator machine is not easy because it is gross. I have done this for clients/patients many times, I do, get nauseated. I have taken care of many dying people in my forty-nine years of caring for people.

The thing I did most was I prayed to God for help and guidance on how to deal and figure out how to solve a problem that has happened. How to correct a mistake, and learn from my mistakes. I have dealt with some smelly stench that just makes me want to quit doing this work. I learned about the use of Vicks VapoRub. Put a little bit of the ointment under my nose. It takes away the repelling smells and odors. It works!

You, the care giver must take care of yourself while working with a dying person. You must eat nourishing foods. Drink a lot of water, to keep hydrated. You must rest when you can. You have to be alert, all the time, when you are working with a dying client/patient. Usually when a client/patient is in the end state of life, there will have to be two or more care givers. Usually this is a twelve-hour shift for each care giver. The time can go fast when there is lot to do.

Quiet music is very comforting to dying clients/patients. It is a distraction that allows the client/patient to forget for the moment the pain of what he/she is going through. Music is solace for the soul.

CHAPTER 15

Documentation

What is documentation? It is a journal or a history that furnishes information, proof, or support of something.

When there is care giving of any sort done to a person, a client/patient, it must be written down in a documentation journal. When you help the client/patient in the morning, put the time he/she wakes up. When the client/patient eats at each meal, and has snacks, write down the time and what the client/patient ate, in the documentation journal. When you give medications, write down the time and name of medicine, in the documentation journal. When dressing the client/patient, and changing the diapers, write the time in the documentation journal. Everything you do for that day must be documented.

Feeding and eating: When you fix and cook food, and the client/patient eats his/her food. When you have to spoon/fork feed a client/patient. This needs to be documented. You have to document everything you feed and cook for the client/patient. Be very detailed about the amounts of food, how much the client/patient ate. Did the client/patient have any problems swallowing the food. Was there any chocking on water and food. The most important is what time each of these was. The doctors and nurses need the information so that he/she can record the information in the patient's medical records.

Bathing and personal hygiene: All bathing and toiletries, toilet use should be documented. All diaper changes must be put into the documentation journal, of the amount of urine, type of fesses, (hard, small, runny, diarrhea, bloody, etc.) All of this tells the doctors and nurses what is going on with the client/patient, and this is recorded in the medical records of the patient. Write down the time and date of the bathing and diaper changes.

Sleep and wake up times: As soon as the client/patient wakes up in the morning, write down the time and date in the documentation journal. If the client/patient needs to have his/her vitals done, take the blood pressure counts and record the numbers in the documentation journal. Blood glucose test taken before breakfast. Record the numbers in the documentation journal. Have the client/patient get on the scale to get the weight number of pounds, record this in the documentation journal.

Medications: Always document all medicine that the client/patient takes. Vitamins and herbs the client takes. Record this in the documentation journal.

Talk to your client/patient and ask how he/she is feeling today. What's on his/her mind. What needs he/she may need done, or want. Document this in the documentation journal.

Document the behaviors of the client/patient. Is he/she moody, depressed nervous, has anxiety, or anxious? Is he/she abusive, complaining, feeling pain, lonely, forgetful, or angary? Does he/she feel tired, slow moving? Is he/she feeling high, manic, or feeling low? Is he/she afraid of something, boisterous and loud, or yelling?

Just remember to be observant and watchful. Record what is happening to the client/patient, in the documentation journal.

There should be instructions that the doctors give, and the home health nurses have for the client/patient. Know what needs to be done for the client/patient. Always remember to read the instructions every day. Record the instructions you have done for the client/patient for the day in the documentation journal.

If there are any changes to the instructions of the procedure care for the client/patient, put that into the documentation journal. If there are any questions you need to know about, call the doctor's nurse, or ask the home health nurses. Any previous care givers should share the information to the new care giver. Document all conversations from the doctors and the home care nurses.

When you get ready to go home after taking care of the client/patient, give all the information to the new care giver that is coming in to work, discuss all the information needed to the care giver. The outgoing care giver signed out and the time signed out. The new care giver signs in and the time signed in.

Shift changes should be documented in the documentation journal.

If you work for a care giving company or an agency, or a medical facility be sure you fill out all the documentation your employers want you to do.

If you work for a medical facility, hospital, or a skilled care nursing home, please follow the companies' instructions and rules on documentation.

The reason for documentation is to history the Client's/patient's progress under your care. Documentation can be used for legal, medical, and family use. Documenting saves you a lot of trouble, fear, and loss of a job. Be sure you write clearly and completely, with good spelling and grammar. Take your time putting the information needed for the documentation journal.

There is an example of the Documentation Journal for the care giver below.

DOCUMENTATION JOURNAL

Patient's name, Date of birth

Date:
Wake up time:
Temperature:
Weight:
Blood Pressure:
Blood glucose Level:
Medications and times taken:

Breakfast meal:
Activities:

Naps and times taken:

Lunch:

Miscellaneous:

Dinner meal:
Bathing:

Hygiene/Personal care:

Diaper changes:
　　Bowel movements:
　　Urination:

Bed time:

Bed bound client/patient Turn times every two hours:

Travel to Doctors appointments, Physical Therapy, shopping:

Care giver comments: If more information is needed, add a sheet of paper to the document information:

Care giver leaving Name and time:

Next shift care giver Name and time:

This is a photograph of my St. Francis of Assisi,
With affirmations on bee bops.

Prayer of Saint Francis of Assisi

Lord, Make me an instrument of your peace,
Where there is hatred, let me sew love;
Where there is injury, pardon;
Where there is doubt, faith;
Where there is despair, hope;
Where there is darkness, light;
Where there is sadness, joy.
O Divine Master,
Grant that I may not so much seek to be consoled,
as to console;
To be understood, as to understand;
To be loved, as to love;
For it is in giving that we receive;
It is in pardoning that we are pardoned;
And it is in dying
that we are born to eternal life.
Amen

FB

CHAPTER 16

Help for the Care Giver

*I shall Take one day at a time.
By Diana Davis*

The care giver is the most important person in taking care of the sick and the elderly. Care givers are vital for the many tasks that have to be done within a given day. The care giver is the first person that the client/patient sees in the morning when he/she gets up, and gets out of the bed. The care giver is the last person the client/patient sees when he/she goes to bed at night. It is important to smile in the morning, and smile at night. Smiles make people happy, and it lifts up the continence of the care giver. Friendliness and smiles mix together like a marriage. They get along with the people you are around with. Who can't feel good when somebody smiles at him/her? Smiles makes the frown go away.

Care givers work long, busy days that are full of many responsibilities, and duties. He/she will start early in the morning before the client/patient wakes up. This regimen of work can involve a work schedule that can last for many days, and possibly weeks. If a family member is the care giver, the days will be long and worrisome for him/her. Many families have care giver relatives that give much time and energy to the family member needing help. Most of the time there is no one else to take care of the family member that is sick, and has a handicap. This care giver may never get paid for his/her work with the family member. The siblings seem to forget, or just don't want to take the responsibility, to take care of the family member that needs the help. This situation leads to total burnout, and health issues start to crop up, because of the stress, and the lack of consideration, that the siblings have given to him/her. When this happens, this is when someone from an outside care giving agency or company, will come in to take care of the client/patient. This man/woman will be paid for his/her services as a professional care giver.

Family members have the highest burnout rate of care givers. His/her time is spent dealing with all the preparation, and taking care of the many appointments, that the sick or handicap family member has to go to. Seeing the parent, child or sibling's health getting worse, from the disease, and sickness, is very sorrowful, and draining to the family care giver, that has the responsibility, and total care of the family member. There could be arguments with the loved one, and the family care giver, who is in charge of the care of the sick family member. The power of attorney in the family needs to be contacted, to come over and speak to the sick family member. Also, to resolve the differences between the family, and discuss the need, that the rest of the family needs to step up and do his/her duty to help take care of the sick family member.

If you have a defiant client/patient who refuses to cooperate and work with you, you will have to work out some boundaries and make a mutual agreement with the client/patient. Otherwise ask for help from the power of attorney, to step in to talk to the client/patient. Sit with the client/patient and find out what he/she is willing to agree to. This client/patient will feel like he/she is losing control and can't be self-sufficient and independent like he/she used to be. The client/patient feels like he/she is losing his/her freedom. Such clients/patients can be very stressful to deal with, and get along with. Give him/her space and time-outs. Do not follow him/her around the house. If you need to follow the client/patient, have a little space between you and the client/patient. Use your best judgement.

There are several working shifts in a twenty-four-hour day, depending on the required duties. The schedule of the working family member, and the condition of the client/patient determines what needs to be done. These shifts are shared among the family members, or there will be a professional care giver coming in to take care of the client/patient.

A four-hour shift is mainly for giving baths, cooking, and feeding the client his/her meals. There might be some light housekeeping, like changing the bedding and doing laundry. This shift might also include when the client/patient has a doctor appointment, or needs to go shopping for the necessary things that are needed.

An eight-hour shift is primarily for the convenience of the working family member. The care giver comes in to take over the care of the client/patient. The family member is freed up to go and do the necessary things without worrying about his/her parent, child, or sibling. The work involves doing many of the things done on a four-hour shift schedule. If the client/patient is able to move around, the care giver may watch the client/patient more so that he/she doesn't have a trip or a fall, or getting into things that he/she should not be into. A dementia or an Alzheimer's clients/patients have to be watch frequently as he/she will get outside and run off, and forget were he/she lives. The care giver will be franticly looking to find this client/patient. Another thing that is common is that the busy client/patient, he/she will get into the refrigerator, to find food to eat all day long. You have to put a stop to that, as the refrigerator will be empty by the time the working family member comes home. Many times, the refrigerator is locked up with a chain, and a padlock. You will have to talk to the family member to get permission to have the key to the padlock, and the location of the padlock key that is hidden, so that the busy client/patient can't find the key to unlock the padlock. The care giver will be a companion most of the time to the client/patient.

A twelve-hour shift is a typical shift to work with a client/patient that is in a more critical condition. This shift is half of the twenty-four-hour shift. You come in the morning to work the day shift and do all the work of the four-hour shift and the eight-hour day shift. When you come in to work the night shift you will be doing night work. That is getting the client ready for bed, brushing his/her teeth. Giving night medications to the client/patient. If the client/patient sleeps all night without any incidences, then you can rest for a while. Have an alarm clock set every hour to check on the client/patient during the night. Many times, the client/patient will get up and walk around the house and go to the bathroom. When this happens just sit with the client/patient and talk with him/her, read a book, and watch television for a while. The twenty-four-hour shift requires two or more care givers to work with the client/patient. Many times, when the client/patient is in a high alert state and he/she is dying, you will be awake all night. You will be very busy, checking on the client/patient. This is really a long night of stress. It is encouraged that this client/patient needs two care givers. It takes two care givers to move the client/patient in different positions in the bed.

The morning shift care giver is responsible for feeding the client/patient, changing his/her clothes. Generally getting the client/patient ready for the day. Take the vitals that are needed, such as the blood pressure, and blood glucose test, and the temperature reading, and giving medications to the client/patient.

The night shift care giver is responsible for getting the vitals that are needed from the client, such as blood pressure, and the blood glucose test. Giving the night medications to the client/patient. Getting the client/patient ready for bed. The night person is responsible for staying up all night. The care giver needs to check on the client frequently and monitor the vitals. Changing the diaper if it is wet and dirty. Helping the client/patient get comfortable in the bed.

Clients/patients will try to get out of bed by himself/herself. Some will work really hard at getting out of bed. If he/she does get out of bed, you will have to help them back into the bed. Don't try to move clients/patients out of bed by yourself, if the client/patient is too weak and heavy to move, have another person help you move the client.

When you are working long shifts, try to get up and move your body often. Sitting too much is very tiring, and it is not good for you to be sitting so much. The muscles cramp when they are not moving often enough. Be active. When the client/patient is sleeping and he/she is calm, you can step out of the room. Go get a drink of water. Eat something. Go to the bathroom. Wash your face with cold water, to keep you awake on the night shift. Get a wash rag and put warm water on it. Wring out the water from the wash rag, put this warm wash rag onto your eyes. This will help your eyes feel better, also, it will help keep you awake. You can step outside and take a breath of fresh air. This will help you stay awake. Walk around the inside of the house. You can exercise often in short quick movements. I like to exercise by the kitchen sink. I have something to hold onto while I stretch my back; and kick up my legs. You can do standing pushups, deep knee bends, etc. Drink ice water with lemon juice. This will help you stay awake. Just think cold to stay awake.

The live-in shift. This shift is a twenty-four-seven shift. That is twenty-four hours a day, for seven days of work. This shift can last more than seven days, sometimes two weeks or more working. This live-in shift is more like a companion shift. The client/patient may be active and move around the house easily. He/she is someone that likes to have company and to do things with. Many of these clients/patients don't like to be alone, especially at night. There may be some health issues, but the health is manageable. Each day encourage the client/patient to go for walks. This keeps the body from getting weak and helps with the balance issues. The client/patient may need a walker or a cane to walk. The reason for this is the client/patient may have dizziness, vertigo, and other balance problems. This is extremely important that the walker, cane, and any other walking assistant tools are used. This will help prevent any falls. When you walk with your client/patient be a step or two behind him/her. This is because, if the client/patient loses his/her balance you are able to prevent the fall or a trip. What you do is, have your hand on the back of the client's/patient's shirt, sweater, or a coat. This will help to prevent a fall. I have done this many times and saved a client/patient from landing on the ground hurt. Another reason you stand back a few steps, is that the client could lose his/her balance and fall against you. You will lose your balance and fall onto the ground, and your client/patient will follow landing on top of you. This has happened to me once. I broke my upper arm femur, and the top part of my arm. I had three broken places on my arm. This happened to me because I wasn't paying attention to the client/patient. This was a very painful lesson I learned.

Here is some advice I'm going to give you so that you will stay healthy, happy, and have a positive experience as a care giver.

When you are working for many hours a day and working a week or two without leaving to go home, you will start to feel overwhelmed, and get cranky too. This is common with people. Stress is caused because you are tired, and you have worked trying to stay nice, caring and kind. Being nice all the time without any time off can get old fast, and you are beginning to think negatively, and just not happy. When you have these kinds of feelings, it is time to stop, and excuse yourself to go to the bathroom. While you are in the bathroom, take the time to relax for five minutes.

Go into the kitchen and cook a meal for yourself and your client/patient. While you are doing the cooking, the client/patient can relax watching the television, maybe he/she is watching his/her favorite game shows, or a soap opera. What this does is giving you time to have some space, and alone time from the client/patient. While you are in the kitchen, eat something while you are cooking, it is ok to do this. Check on the client/patient every ten or fifteen minutes to be sure he/she is ok. Maybe bring him/her a glass of tea, or some other beverage. This helps the client/patient know that you are thinking of him/her while you're in another room cooking dinner.

You need to learn how to think differently, and change the repetitive negative thoughts into some happy thoughts. Think of a time that you really had so much fun, when you were young. It can be anything. After thinking the happy thoughts, you will start smiling, and maybe laughing out loud. Laughter is really good for you. This helps lift up the joy feeling in your body.

When you and your client are watching television together, try to find something that is funny to watch. Both of you will have a good time doing this together. Take turns watching a show that you like, and that the client/patient will like too. Share life experiences together. Clients/patients love to talk about his/her life, and ambitions, family, and trips, just talk about anything that the two of you want to talk about. A caution, don't talk about troublesome things, and your deep private things. Clients/patients have a tendency to think about things, and he/she will internalize the thoughts, to where he/she thinks it is his/her own problem.

When the client/patient takes a nap, you take a nap. When the client goes to bed for the night, you go to bed for the night. The secret to good health is a good sleep and being rested.

Take frequent breaks during the day. Remember you are a live-in care giver, and you are working for days on end, until you get a relief care giver to come to work after you. You are not a machine. You are not a slave. You are a beautiful, handsome, wonderful, ambitious, talented human being. You are worthy to take time off during the day, and sleep at nights without being coursed into doing, and never-ending doing. There is time to do things, and a time to play, and a time to rest. This is a key I am giving you so that you last out the full working shift.

Before you go on the job, pack your suitcase with what you will need for a week. First pack your own pillow, (you don't want to sleep on other people's night mares). Pack a teddy bear, or a stuff heart pillow. I know it sound crazy but I'm telling you this will help you when you are feeling down. Pack your pajamas, change of clothes, and clean underpants, and a bra. Men you don't wear a bra, I know that. Have a housecoat, and a towel of your own to use when taking a shower or a bath. You might want to bring your own sheets. Yes, sometime the bedding for care givers is horrible and dirty. Bring books to read. Bring your hobbies with you, like knitting, crocheting, and puzzles, to do with your client/patient if you want to.

I encourage you to get up an hour earlier than your client/patient, because you need time to wake up in a positive mood. When you are rushed before you are awake, this makes for the start of a stressful day. You need to think of ways to keep the day positive. Get a notebook or a journal to help you plan your day. If you do journaling, do it in the morning and at night before going to bed. This is your private journal. There is a journal that is provided for you to use at the back part of the book.

The next thing you need to do is get dressed for the day. Go into the kitchen and get the coffee pot going. The smell of coffee in the morning is heavenly. If the client/patient is a tea drinker, heat up some water, and pour a cup of hot water into a mug or tea cup, with the tea bag in the cup. This will be ready when the client/patient comes into the kitchen. If you feel that you should eat by yourself, go ahead, and eat your breakfast before the client/patient comes in. Many clients/patients like having someone with him/her to eat meals together. There are a lot of great conversations to have, talking over a meal.

When you get dressed for the day, try to wear loose, comfortable clothing. Most care givers wear scrubs. Scrubs are part of the uniform that nurses and CNA's wear. The scrub top has pockets, and the pants have pockets too. Pockets are a life saver when you need to have extra hands to take care of your client/patient. When you are moving the client/patient, you can put the things in your pockets that you will need for the work you are going to be doing. Things like pencils, scissors, tubes of hand lotion, hair brush. Just about anything you can think of can go into a pocket. Pants can be stretchy pants that give and stretch when you bend down, kneel, and move around. I like wearing stretch pants. Many care givers wear cotton scrub tops, and stretchy pants.

Wear comfortable shoes that have rubber soles so that you don't slip and fall. You need shoes that are stable and sturdy as you will need stability when you are assisting the client/patient.

When you style your hair, try to keep it out of your face. This can be a nerve raking hindrance when you are working and assisting your client/patient. This can be dangerous because you could lose the control to hold on to your client/patient because when your hair gets into your face, you automatically try to swipe the hair off from your face.

When you wear jewelry, try to wear small size jewelry. When you wear long hanging earrings, you risk the chance of getting your earring caught under something. This will pull the earring off your ear, or your earlobe will get ripped. Large rings are pretty but they get in the way and can scratch the client/patient, or they will get caught into the fibers of towels and other bulky, loopy fabrics. Small bracelets are ok as long as there are no charms hanging on them. The charms fall off too easy if they are pulled. Bangle and stretchy bracelets are ok as they hug to the wrist. Always have a watch, with a second hand on it, this will help you identify the time when something happens. A flexible band is a better band to wear because it stretches to your wrist movement. Make sure the watch is water resistant.

Laugh a lot. Laughing helps relieve a lot of stress. When you laugh, you take in a lot of air into your lungs, and you breathe deeper. Laughing makes the brain give off endorphins, this is the happy-feeling chemical that makes you feel good.

When you are watching television with your client/patient, have ear plugs. As people get older, he/she loses his/her hearing. The television is turned up as loud as it can get. So, protect your hearing.

If the client/patient has a baby monitor, use it. Put the baby monitor in the client's/patient's room near the bed, so that you can keep tabs on the client/patient, if the/she is resting and sleeping well. This will free your mind from worrying about if the client/patient is sleeping or trying to call you for help.

There are many kinds of baby monitors available. Video monitors are great if you have a client/patient who likes to get out of bed and walk around the house. Talk to the power of attorney about getting a baby monitor, to listen for movements of the client/patient. These monitors can save your client's/patient's life because you can see and hear his/her call for help.

When you feel anxiety and fear creeping up on you, stop what you are doing and go sit down for a short while. Write down what is happening around you that is causing you to feel like this. Figure out what happened during the day that triggered this feeling. Did you feel threatened in any way? Sometimes the client's/patient's family members can make you feel anxious and threatened. Have they talked down to you? Have they demeaned you? Has there been a lot of disrespectful behavior from the family members towards you? Have you been abused in any way? This could be assaulted, insulted, physical abuse, sexual abuse, mental abuse, threats of harm to you. Abuse and assault are a reason to leave a job. You are not there to be the family punching bag. You can report them to your agency or company you work for. If you are self-employed, you can quit that job, and report the abuse to the police. No job is worth it when there is abuse. The fear you feel is the loss of money. The worry is fear.

Job burnout is very common among care givers. Some of the symptoms of a job burnout are insomnia, restlessness, headaches, heartburn, indigestion, tremors, or shaking in different parts of the body, twitching eyes, or feeling that your heart is racing or pounding in your chest, as well as losing your voice, biting your fingernails, and co-dependent behaviors. You may experience worry, fear of financial loss, and fear of losing your job. Some care givers have high blood pressure, and don't know it until he/she feels like they have a heart attack, or anxiety. Anxiety can feel like a heart attack. If you are experiencing the job burnout problem, I suggest you to visit the doctor, and have counseling.

You must be balanced in your body, and your mind. When you are out of balance, and feeling bad, and sick, all of this affects your spirit. Feeling bad for a long time, gets to you and you start thinking negative thoughts. Try to be positive in your thinking. What we think, we become. Our thoughts affect our actions, and our actions affect what we are thinking.

Talk to yourself in a positive way. What comes out of the mouth is power. Your words have power that can cause you to heal or cause you to hurt and be sick. There is power in the tongue, this tongue of yours can be a tremendous asset of your life, or it can bring you down and destroy you. <u>You must think before you speak</u>. This wisdom will help you in life in getting along with people. When you're being bombarded by someone, trying to get you upset and angry, pressing your buttons into anger, you are getting upset, you automatically speak without thinking. Then later, you really regret what you have said to that person you spoke to. The next time this kind of situation happens to you, just leave the room, or house so that you can be alone to calm down.

Injuries on the Job

You may get injured while taking care of your client/patient. You need to give yourself unconditional love when you are injured. You need to see the doctor, or go to the hospital, to determine the extent of the injuries, from any accident or a fall that you had, while working on the job. Bones can be broken during falls. You will not have any strength because the support of the bone is weakened because it is broken. You can't lift or try to move anything. If you have a broken limb, it will just hang loosely and hurting really bad. You will have tears. When a bone breaks, it sounds like a bag full of crackers being crushed. You can hear a bone break. This is an emergency, visit to the hospital. Don't delay going to the hospital to get treated.

Any cuts, and abrasions that you get while on the job should be taken care of. Deep cuts that are in need of stitches need to be dealt with. Go to the doctor or hospital. When you have cuts, put pressure on the cut, use a paper towel or cotton gauze to cover the cut, put pressure on the cut to stop the bleeding. When the bleeding has stopped, put antibacterial ointment on the cut, and cover with a band aid.

You will have to report to your employer the injuries you have sustained. Journal in the documentation journal of any of this kind of injuries of yourself. Call the power of attorney or guardian, to let him/her know that you are injured, and that your employer is getting a replacement care giver, to take care of the client/patient.

As I end this chapter, Help for the Care giver. I want you to remember the advice and the wisdom I have given you. As the years go by, you can reflect on the experiences that you had in working as a care giver. What you have done in life, in taking care of people, and reaching out with the great love you have for people. What you have accomplished in life. Just remember that you are unique and special, with many talents and abilities. Some things that you have done were good, and some things not so good. That is life. We learn as we go in life. We learn from our mistakes and learn what works best for us. Trust in yourself. Believe in yourself. Have faith in yourself. Compliment yourself for the many people you have taken care of. Believe that you are good, and you have the gift of love, to share with the suffering people who inhabit this world. You are on a mission for God, to take care of the sick, the hungry, and the needy. Care giving is a calling from God.

It takes a lot of understanding and intuitiveness to care for people. It takes a lot of prayer and seeking for answers to solve situations. It takes believing, to ask God, and the angels for help, and guidance on how to solve the many problems that occur, during the time that you care for your client/patient.

Prayer is the soul's sincere desire. Prayer solves many situations and problems. Prayer gives you supernatural strength, to fill the needs you have, and to accomplish the healing you need, when you hurt.

CHAPTER 17

Meditations

*Meditate gratitude,
I am thankful,
Thank you.
By
Diana Davis*

This is an Passion flower from my garden

Meditation is to muse or have intuition about something, contemplate and think about something, ponder is to consider a problem or a study, to engage in deep mental exercise, to imagine possibilities.

Meditation has been practiced for thousands of years. Meditation is commonly used for relaxation and stress reduction.

Meditation is a type of mind-body relaxation medicine to help reduce stress that is caused from trauma, post-traumatic-stress disorder. Meditation can produce a deep state of relaxation and a tranquil mind.

During meditation, you will focus your attention on one thing. Eliminate the stream of monkey-mind thoughts that may be crowding your mind and causing stress. This process may result in enhanced physical and emotional well-being.

The benefit of meditation can give you a sense of calmness, peace, and balance that can benefit both your emotional well-being, and your overall health. You can use meditation to relax, and cope with stress. You can focus your attention on calming thoughts. Meditation can help your inner peace. It can help carry you more calmly throughout your day. Meditation may help you manage symptoms of certain medical conditions.

Breathing Meditation

Slowly breath in four counts,
Hold for four counts,
release your breath for four counts.
Repeat this several times until you feel calm.

Walking Meditation

Put on some comfortable walking shoes, warm up your legs and feet, by stretching your legs and feet. Put your right foot forward about a foot. Put your left foot behind you about a foot. Bend your right knee forward and hold. Keep your left foot flat on the ground. Hold this for 5 counts. Repeat this with the left leg forward, and the right foot behind you. You can repeat this stretching several times, until you feel relaxed and loosened up.

When you are done warming up your legs and feet. Start walking and breathing in the fresh outside air. Look around you, and just be relaxed. No hurry, no rushing things. This is your time to just be. Hear the bird's chirp. Look at the colors of the trees, and plants. Stop, and smell the flowers. Slowly walk, and while you walk, move your arms back and forth, keeping pace with your legs. While you are walking, look at the ground around you. You might find an interesting rock, to put into your rock collection. Pickup a pine cone or a stick, whatever gets your attention, and it's something you like.

When you are ready to go home. Turn around and walk back home. Smile.

Singing Meditation

Singing is so good for you. When you sing, you are taking a deep breath, and then releasing sound, (sing), as you breathe out. You can sing any kind of song you want. While you are singing, listen to the sound of your voice, feel your voice flow through your vocal cords, up through your mouth and out. Wiggle your tongue while you are singing. Sing the songs that you love. Funny kids' songs, hymn songs, love songs, and have fun doing this. You can turn on the cd's, or play vintage black-vinyl records, just turn up the volume on the phonograph, and sing along with the songs. Just have fun, you don't have to be at perfect pitch while singing. No perfection or feeling self-conscious is aloud.

Meditative Dancing

Meditative dancing is very relaxing, and it is fun to do. Put on some music, either from your cell phone or from a CD. Move your body along with the beat of the music. Raise your arms up and wide open, and lean your head back, like you're looking at the sky, or the ceiling. If you have good balance, you can close your eyes, and just move your body. You can do this meditative dancing as long as you want. There is no time limit. When you are done, you will feel wonderful, and light hearted. You can use any kind of music that appeals to you.

Progressive Relaxation Meditation

Progressive relaxation meditation is a very good way to release stress and anxiety. You need to do this meditation slowly, so that you can benefit from this meditation. You can do this meditation while you are lying on the floor, on your bed, or outside on the lawn. Were ever you wish to do this. This is also fun to do by a creek because you can hear the water flowing down the creek. You can find meditation music with sounds of nature. I recommend this because the sounds help you go into a deeper relaxed state of the mind, body, and your spirit.

Take a deep breath, and slowly let it out. Start relaxing from the bottoms of your feet, and relax gradually up your body to the top of your head.

Take a deep breath, through your nose. slowly release your breath, out through your mouth.

Each time you change the muscle group, do the deep breaths sequences.

Tighten your muscles around your feet. Hold for five seconds, relax your feet.

Take a deep breath, through your nose, slowly release your breath, out through your mouth.

Tighten your calve muscles, hold for five seconds, relax your calve muscles.

Take a deep breath, through your nose, slowly release your breath, out through your mouth.

Tighten your thigh muscles, hold for five seconds, relax your thigh muscles.

Take a deep breath, through your nose, slowly release your breath, out through your mouth.

Tighten your buttock muscles, hold for five seconds, relax your buttocks muscles.

Take a deep breath, through your nose, slowly release your breath, out through your mouth.

Tighten your stomach muscles, hold for five seconds, relax your stomach muscles.

Take a deep breath, through your nose, slowly release your breath, through your mouth.

Tighten your chest muscles, hold for five seconds, release your chest muscles.

Take a deep breath, through your nose, slowly release your breath, through your mouth.

Tighten your shoulder muscles, hold for five seconds, release your shoulder muscles.

Take a deep breath, through your nose, slowly release your breath, through your mouth.

Tighten your arms and hands muscles, hold for five seconds, release your arms and hands muscles.

Take a deep breath, through your nose, slowly release your breath, through your mouth.

Tighten your face muscles, hold for five seconds, release your face muscles.

Take a deep breath, through your nose, slowly release your breath, through your mouth.

You should feel very relaxed and calmer after this meditation. You will likely fall asleep for a while. That is ok. You needed the sleep. When you get up after doing this progressive relaxation meditation, you need to get up slowly. Stretch your body and enjoy the rest of your day.

CHAPTER 18

Affirmations

Photograph by Diana Davis

Affirmations are really good to do each day. By repeating the daily affirmations, your mind and thoughts start to change. Affirmations are great when you are starting to feel down in the mouth, and negative. You can change this negative self-talk and start seeing results slowly changing to the positive self-talk, and feeling more positive about yourself, and about many things in your life.

Try to say the affirmations every day. Say the affirmations in the morning when you wake up, and say the affirmations when you go to bed. When you're out of sorts, say the affirmations several times a day.

In time, you will see a change come over you in your life. This is a life changing behavior healing. Remember, what you think of yourself, be it true or false, will affect your life in many areas. Your relationships with people will become happier, and more positive. Your working life will be more positive, because you are using a powerful tool that changes things to the good positive. You will go through life feeling you have confidence, and a power of inner strength that gets you through situations that can be difficult to go through.

There are many ways that you can say your affirmations. You can stand in front of the mirror, and say your affirmations, while you are looking at yourself. It's surprising how this works, and I believe it is because when you look at yourself, saying a positive thing about yourself is healing to the mind but also your spirit. When you look into your eyes, in the mirror, this is a real powerful truth, you are receiving from yourself. Your deep mind self, the subconscious mind. Affirmations work by sinking into the deep thought part of the brain, the subconscious mind.

You may want to journal your experiences, while saying your affirmations. Write intuitive thoughts that come to you, when you are expressing the affirmations. You can get flashcards, and you write your affirmations on the cards, then use those cards when you are working, and at home. Flash cards are an amazing tool to use. Make up some of your own affirmations. You will be surprised how many affirmations you can make up for yourself.

AFFIRMATIONS

1. I am relaxed, and I go with the flow.
2. My day is beautiful, and full of joy.
3. I am intelligent.
4. I know how to give love and care.
5. I am a great care giver.
6. I am doing well for myself.
7. I love myself fully, and completely.
8. I go with the flow, and I ride the tide to my goals.
9. When I feel challenged, I say my affirmations more.
10. I love my clients, and they love me too.
11. I am strong and healthy.
12. I breathe with joy, and I am happy.
13. I wake up feeling completely rested.
14. Every day is a beautiful day for me.
15. I embrace the sun each day.

16. I absorb the warm sun-beam's healing touch.
17. I trust the process of life.
18. I am worthy to receive, all the goodness in life.
19. Life is good to me. Thank you.
20. I am grateful, that I live.

My Biography

Diana Davis and Yoda

I am the author of my second book, "Guide for the Care Giver." My first book I wrote was, "Wise Advice for Caregivers." After working for almost fifty years, I am now a retired senior citizen and care giver. I have more to teach you, and show you, as throughout the years since I wrote my first book, I have learned a lot more information about the care giving field, and now I am sharing with you my readers, what I know.

I have written short stories, poems, and small documentaries on my favorite subjects. I like taking photographs and writing stories about the pictures. I have been a care giver since I was nineteen years old. I have worked off and on in the care giving field. I have done private care giving, self-employed care giving, and I have worked for companies that employed care givers. I have worked in memory care facility homes, taking care of people that had Alzheimer's disease, and dementia memory loss.

When I was nineteen years old, I married my first husband, Charles. Charles was a large man; he was paralyzed from his waist to his feet. This was caused by having Polio-meningitis when he was a child. I had to learn how to take care of him, when he needed me to help him, in the various things he had to do. I had to maneuver him into the wheelchair, lift him into a shower stall, lift him into a bath tub. Assist him into a car and assist him to sit in regular furniture. There was no information on how to take care of people. There were no books, or videos about how to take care of people, that was handicap challenged, and disabled.

As the years went by, I had people requesting me to help them with the needs of his/her family, parents, children. People with disabilities called me, asking for my help. To give him/her baths and dress him/her.

I have worked in the medical field for many years as a receptionist, to check in patients for his/her doctor appointment. I made medical record histories for patients. I was a phlebotomist, drawing blood from patients. I also worked in the laboratory, as a lab technician, processing blood specimens, and many other specimens that had to get processed, and to be sent to other laboratories, for the results to come back to the ordering doctors, that needed the results of the tests.

I have been proactive in the care of my clients/patients and seeing how the improvements that the clients/patients went through, in the process of getting well. I have seen many clients/patients win his/her freedom from being in bed. To get out of bed walking, talking, and literally stepping outside of the home, and be in the sun light, for the first time in days, months, and even years, of being a prisoner of his/her bed.

I have studied many subjects in my life, and the two subjects that helped me to understand people were psychology and sociology. I have read and studied many books on self-care, to help myself first but also to understand how to help others. I have studied music and learn how to play the piano at the age of nineteen. When I was in my early twenties, I played the piano in church, for weddings, and children's ministries. I have studied the Cello, and I played the Cello in the California State University string orchestra. I have learned to play many different instruments, throughout the years in my life. I have studied Horticulture, the study of plants, through the library system. I love gardening and grow exotic plants. I am a musician, artist, homemaker, seamstress, Gardener, and an author. I love to create things, and make beautiful works of art for my home, and also to give away as gifts, for my friends, and family.

RESOURCES

Merriam-Webster Dictionary, Printed August 1974. Pocket Books, a division of Simon and Schuster, Inc. 1230 Avenue of the Americas, New York, New York. USA 10020

Roget's Thesaurus. Ballantine Publishing Group 1998. Random House, Inc., 201 East 50th St., New York, New York. USA 10022

Winter, Griffith H. *Complete Guide to Symptoms, Illness, and Surgery. 6th Edition, December 2012.* Body Press, Penguin Group (USA) Inc. 375 Hudson St., New York, New York. USA 10014

Hay, Louise L. You Can Heal Your Life. 1999, Hay House Inc. P.O. Box5100, Carlsbad, Ca. 92018-5100

Davis, Diana S. Wise Advice for Caregivers, 2015, Balboa Press, A Division of Hay House, 1663 Liberty Drive, Bloomington, IN 47403

New American Standard Bible, Zondervan Publishing House, 5300 Patterson Ave. SE, Grand Rapids, MI.

NRV Holy Bible, New Revised Standard Version, Catholic Edition, Anglicized Text, Catholic Bible Press, Harper Collins Christian Publishers, P O Box 141000, Nashville, TN, 37214

King James Version Bible, Zondervan Publishing House, 5300 Patterson Ave. SE, Grand Rapids, MI.

Jacobs, Michael B M.D., *Taking Care,* Department of Veterans Affairs, 4100 East Mississippi Ave., Glendale, Co. 80222 Random House, New York.

Davis, Diana S. *Artwork, drawings, photographs,* Evanston, Wyoming.

www.WebMD.com

www.MayoClinic.com

www.AARP.org

www.goggle.com, *Royalty free images and illustrations.*

RECOMMENDED READING

Hay, Louise L. *You Can Heal Your Life*. Hay House, Inc., P. O. Box 5100, Carlsbad, Ca. 92018

Hay, Louise L., and Davis Kessler. *You can Heal Your Heart*. Hay House, Inc., P. O. Box 5100, Carlsbad, Ca. 92018

Jacobs, Michael B M.D., *Taking Care,* Department of Veterans Affairs, 4100 East Mississippi Ave., Glendale, Co. 80222 Random House, New York.

Maisel, Eric PHD, *Overcoming Your Difficult Family,* 2017, New World Library, 14 Pamaron Way, Novato, Ca. 94949

Dyer, Wayne W. Dr., *Change Your Thoughts-Change Your Life. 2007,* Hay House, Inc., P. O. Box 5100, Carlsbad, Ca. 92018

Dyer, Wayne W. Dr., *You'll See It When You Believe It 1989,* Hay House, Inc., P. O. Box 5100, Carlsbad, Ca. 92018

New American Standard Bible, Zondervan Publishing House, 5300 Patterson Ave. SE, Grand Rapids, MI.

AARP Bulletin, www.AARP.org

AARP Magazine, www.AARP.org

My Journal

My Journal

My Journal

My Journal

My Journal

My Journal

My Journal

My Journal

My Journal

My Journal

My Journal

My Journal

My Journal

My Journal

My Journal

My Journal

My Journal

My Journal

My Journal

My Journal

My Journal

My Journal

My Journal

My Journal

My Journal

My Journal

www.ingramcontent.com/pod-product-compliance
Lightning Source LLC
LaVergne TN
LVHW020412070526
838199LV00054B/3587